JON SOBRINO

Jon Sobrino

Spiritual Writings

Selected with an Introduction by

ROBERT LASSALLE-KLEIN

ORBIS BOOKS

Maryknoll, New York 10545

ORBIS BOOKS
Maryknoll, New York 10545

Fathers and Brothers
MARYKNOLL

Founded in 1970, Orbis Books endeavors to publish works that enlighten the mind, nourish the spirit, and challenge the conscience. The publishing arm of the Maryknoll Fathers and Brothers, Orbis seeks to explore the global dimensions of the Christian faith and mission, to invite dialogue with diverse cultures and religious traditions, and to serve the cause of reconciliation and peace. The books published reflect the views of their authors and do not represent the official position of the Maryknoll Society. To learn more about Maryknoll and Orbis Books, please visit our website at www.maryknollsociety.org.

Library of Congress Cataloging-in-Publication Data

Names: Sobrino, Jon, author. | Lassalle-Klein, Robert Anthony, editor.
Title: Jon Sobrino : spiritual writings / selected with an introduction by Robert Lassalle-Klein.
Description: Maryknoll : Orbis Books, 2018. | Series: Modern spiritual masters series | Includes bibliographical references.
Identifiers: LCCN 2018020924 (print) | LCCN 2018031478 (ebook) | ISBN 9781608337668 (e-book) | ISBN 9781626983007 (pbk.)
Subjects: LCSH: Christian life--Catholic authors.
Classification: LCC BX4705.S66385 (ebook) | LCC BX4705.S66385 A25 2018 (print) | DDC 230/.2--dc23

LC record available at https://lccn.loc.gov/2018020924

For Jon Sobrino,
witness to the joyful discovery that
God comes to meet humanity
through love for the crucified people
and who once told me,
"I gave up my career and
just wrote what I was asked."

With gratitude and affection:
Bob, Lynn, Kate, Rose,
and Peter Lassalle-Klein

Contents

Foreword

I am surprised and grateful for the interest in a collection of my spiritual writings. At the same time, I rejoice in this book because I believe that the topics addressed here will do some good: God and Jesus of Nazareth, the martyrs, and the victims.

Paradoxically, though all of these are weighty topics, including God, I also believe that each of them generates hope and joy.

I am especially grateful to my friend Robert Lassalle-Klein for this great volume. I hope that his effort to make these texts widely available will bring inspiration and hope to everyone who reads them.

Jon Sobrino
Centro Monseñor Romero
San Salvador

Introduction

> Idols are historical realities today, they promise salvation, they demand orthodoxy and a cult, and they require victims in order to survive, like the god Moloch.
> —Jon Sobrino, *Jesus of Galilee*

> There are hundreds of millions of poor and oppressed in the world, in whom appears what I have called "primordial holiness," seen in their untiring clinging to life, one to another in repressions, wars, migrations, and refugee centers. Miraculously many times they remain hopeful, offer pardon, and search for reconciliation. Moreover, they have a convening power, which generates solidarity, understood as mutual support, giving to one another and receiving one another with the best that one has. Those who come from the world of plenty to help the poor repeatedly say, with thanks, that they have received more than they have given. Therefore, looking at both the world of abundance and the world of poverty, I have said *extra pauperes nulla salus* (outside the poor there is no salvation). Taking one step further, salvation comes from the poor. They are the servant of Yahweh.
> —Jon Sobrino, *The Galilean Jesus*

Over thirty years ago in 1986, as Jon Sobrino spoke about El Salvador to a room of San Francisco–area church people, it occurred to me that my "yes" or "no" to God's invitation to solidarity with the crucified people of El Salvador was drawing me and my fellow citizens inexorably into a *mysterium tremendum et fascinans* of evil and grace. How had I not known about this? We had heard details of the murder of Jon's friend, Archbishop Oscar Romero, as he said Mass, on the orders of Roberto D'Aubuisson, founder of the right-wing Arena Party, which controlled the National Assembly of the US-supported government through

1

the mid1980s. Later, as I drove with Jon to an event at our newly refounded Oakland Catholic Worker, we had discussed whether Jesus was right when he said that God had chosen to meet us in the invitation to compassion for the poor, the imprisoned, the naked, and the hungry (Mt. 25:31–46).

Both new and experienced readers of Jon Sobrino will find fresh questions and insights in the spiritual writings collected here, some of them appearing for the first time. Several go to the heart of what it means to be human in an often inhumane world, while others take the reader inside remarkable friendships, profound joys, and real suffering. Jon Sobrino is perhaps the leading witness and interpreter of the epoch-changing religious and political events that rocked Latin America and the Catholic Church in the decades after World War II. In 1968, the Latin American bishops at Medellín, Colombia, became the first episcopal conference, three years after the close of Vatican II, to officially respond to the call to read the signs of the times in light of the Gospel. Their prayerful conclusion was that God was calling the Latin American church to embrace a "preferential option for the poor" in support of the growing aspirations of the continent's poor majorities for liberation and development.

Years of controversy, debate, and clarification followed, but Pope John Paul II eventually incorporated the preferential option for the poor into the heart of Catholic Social Teaching during his long pontificate (1978–2005). Jon Sobrino and other liberation theologians, however, were vilified, physically threatened, and attacked by economic elites and their friends in the church hierarchy. In the case of Sobrino, this resulted in a "Notification" issued by the Congregation for the Doctrine of the Faith (CDF) on November 26, 2005, warning of "certain impressions and errors" in his two-volume Christology. In this volume Fr. Sobrino has decided to publish for the first time his private December 13, 2006, letter to Fr. Peter Hans Kolvenbach, S.J., Superior General of the Society of Jesus. This letter, previously leaked, but never published by the author himself, details why he could not, in good conscience, sign a statement that he adhered "without reservations" to the criticisms stated in the CDF's document. Sobrino's letter is blunt in its painful recitation of injustices and what he sees as intentional misrepresentations of his work and that of others at the hands of people like Cardinal Lopez-Trujillo, a self-declared enemy of Latin American liberation theology. In the end, the CDF issued a "warning" but no prohibition against writing or teaching, and Pope Francis has recently encouraged Sobrino to "keep writing."

Elsewhere in this volume we hear Sobrino's reflections on Fr. Rutilio Grande, S.J., his rural ministry among the *campesinos* of Aguilares, and the role of his martyrdom in the conversion of Archbishop Oscar Romero. We read firsthand accounts of personal conversations and interactions with (Saint) Oscar Romero. We learn details about the conversion to the option for the poor of the Jesuits of Central America, and everyday conversations about the reign of God among the Jesuits and their coworkers at the University of Central America (UCA). We gain new insights into the heart and mind of the brilliant Ignacio Ellacuría, Sobrino's closest collaborator and friend at the UCA. And we stand with Sobrino by the bodies of the four North American churchwomen murdered in December 1980.

This volume includes very personal reflections from Sobrino on the murder of his friends, six Jesuits and two women, on November 16, 1989, and the role of their loss in his personal life, his spirituality, and his thought. Those who died included Fr. Ignacio Ellacuría, S.J., Rector of the UCA and the country's leading public intellectual; Fr. Martín-Baró, S.J., university vice president for academic affairs and director of the University Institute of Public Opinion (IUDOP); Fr. Segundo Montes, S.J., director of the Human Rights Institute of the UCA (IDHUCA) and superior of the Jesuit community; Fr. Amando López, S.J., professor of theology and philosophy, and ex-president of the UCA in Managua; Fr. Joaquin López y López, S.J., national director of *Fe y Alegría*, an education and direct service program for children in poverty; Fr. Juan Ramón Moreno, S.J., assistant director of the newly constructed Oscar Romero Pastoral Center, campus

home of the Center for Theological Reflection and part of the
Jesuit community; Elba Ramos, cook for one of the seminary
communities; and her sixteen-year-old daughter, Celina. We hear
Sobrino's reflections on the role of the Salvadoran government
in their deaths and the subsequent collapse of US congressio-
nal support for its decade-long campaign of repression of Salvadoran civil society and their civil war against the rebels. In all
of these details and more, the volume provides a rich variety of
insights into Sobrino's inner life and spirituality.

The proceeds from this book will go to the Monseñor Romero
Center, where Sobrino works and the martyrs died. Sobrino was
personally involved in selecting the material for the volume and
enthusiastically agreed that the piece on Dean Brackley, S.J.,
should be the conclusion. Dean Brackley was born on August
9, 1946, in Wynantskill, in upstate New York, the oldest of four
children of J. Dean and Inez Brackley. He entered the Jesuits in
1964 and was ordained a priest in 1976. He earned a doctoral
degree in social ethics from the University of Chicago Divinity
School in 1980 and rejected several full-time academic positions
at Jesuit universities to work with a church-sponsored community organizing project in New York, the South Bronx People
for Change. After almost ten years of shuttling (sometimes on
his bike) between this community and Fordham University to
teach ethics and theology, he volunteered for an international
team of five Jesuits, sent to replace the six Jesuits murdered on
November 16, 1989. Dean had the office next to Sobrino in
the Monseñor Oscar Romero Center until his death of pancreatic cancer on October 16, 2011. But he was often downstairs,
hosting thousands of students and faculty members from North
American Jesuit and other universities who went to El Salvador
in order to honor, understand, and connect to the Jesuit martyrs.
Emails would often reach colleagues in the United States and
elsewhere around the world with time stamps from well past
midnight. Famous for his good humor, patience, and compassion, pilgrims were always sent home with the advice to "let the
poor break your heart."

Brackley became internationally known for his work in social ethics and the Spiritual Exercises of St. Ignatius, receiving a variety of academic honors and invitations for guest lectures. He was an important US Jesuit presence at the UCA, where he held many jobs, including (among others) core faculty for the graduate programs in theology, superior to Jesuits in formation for the priesthood, administrator of the School of Religious Education, and weekend pastor of the diocesan church in Jayaque, an hour-plus bus ride from the UCA. Dean was beloved by El Salvador's common people, whom he treated with the greatest respect and considered it his honor to serve. He was the only one of those missioned to replace the murdered Jesuits who managed to stay, and many considered it a miracle of generosity and grace that he was able to successfully fit in, where others had struggled. During a visit shortly before his death, I said, "It's amazing, Dean, what God has accomplished through you at the UCA, all the thousands of people you have touched, and the good you have done." Typically self-deprecating, he replied, "Well, I just got lucky. After the guys died, I raised my hand and was sent to El Salvador, where I've had a great 21 years." I said, "Well, Dean, God can call, but we have to say, 'yes!'" His energy depleted from the chemotherapy and our visit, Dean closed his eyes as he lay flat on his back, turned his palms toward the sky, and with a smile on his face simply said, "Digo, Sí, Señor!"

Sobrino's article for Dean, which he finished for the October 27, 2011, issue of *Letter to the Churches*, after staying up all night, is cast in the mold of his annual "Letter to Ellacuría." With a nod to its author, Sobrino alters Ellacuría's famous phrase, "With Archbishop Romero, God visited El Salvador," to read, "with Dean Brackley, God visited us." In all previous writings (as far as I know), Sobrino reserves this metaphor for a holy trinity of Salvadoran martyrs: Rutilio Grande, Archbishop Romero, and Ignacio Ellacuría. It is shocking to hear it applied to an outsider, especially a U.S. citizen, and to learn from Sobrino that the Jesuit community had offered to bury Dean in the UCA chapel with the martyrs. Not surprisingly, Dean refused and insisted on being buried in the cemetery with the common Jesuits. Sobrino expressed his admiration for this decision, which he found completely typical for Brackley, and writes to Ellacuría, "Father Dean did not die crucified, but he lived to the end actively participating in the crosses of this world. He worked with *power*, that is, with strength and energy, to take them [the crucified people] down from the cross. And he always thought of himself last. Like the crucified God."[1] Sobrino's deep affection for Brackley is clear when he writes, "Love and gratitude have overflowed in many celebrations with tears and joy in the journey to the cemetery."

In using Ellacuría's revered phrase for Dean Brackley I believe that Sobrino is blessing and thanking the many US citizens who have given so much of their lives to accompany the Salvadoran people. This is a surprising and moving development: that the best of us from the United States should be welcomed onto the UCA's most symbolically sacred ground of love and solidarity with the crucified people. At the same time, this act of love and generosity opens a window on the inner workings of Sobrino's heart and mind, the core of his spirituality, if you will. In my view, it reveals the fact that nationality, international conflicts, and US foreign policy aside, Sobrino's heart really does lie with the crucified people and those who love them.

BIOGRAPHY: AWAKENING FROM THE SLEEP OF INHUMANITY

Jon Sobrino's family fled persecution and war in Bilbao, Spain, before moving to Barcelona in 1937, where he was born the following year and lived until 1950. After studying with the Jesuits at the *Colegio de Sarriá* in Barcelona (1948–50) and *Nuestra Señora de Begoña* in Bilbao (1950–56), he entered the Jesuits on October 6, 1956. One year later, in October 1957, he and several classmates joined Fr. Miguel Elizondo at the new Jesuit novitiate

---

1. Jon Sobrino, "The *Always* of the Crucified People. 'What to Do with the Good Ones.'" "Carta a Ellacuría, Dean Brackley," 25–27.

at *Santa Tecla* in San Salvador, eight years after it began with Ellacuría and his classmates. Following vows, Sobrino undertook undergraduate studies in humanities from 1958 to 1960 with the Jesuit faculty in Havana, Cuba, where the seminarians studied as the Cuban Revolution unfolded, with Fidel Castro and his fellow revolutionaries entering Havana on the morning of January 1, 1959. Sobrino left the island in 1960, just months before the January 1961 announcement that all Jesuit schools would be closed, and the order was expelled in May (one month after the CIA-led Bay of Pigs Invasion).[2] He moved to St. Louis University in Missouri where he completed a B.A. and obtained a licentiate in philosophy in 1963, staying on for a master's in structural engineering, which he completed in 1965. Following graduation, he returned to San Salvador to teach Latin, Greek, and literature at the diocesan seminary (*San José de la Montaña*), and philosophy and mathematics at UCA. One year later he was sent to Frankfurt, Germany, for theological studies at the *Hoch Schule Sankt Georgen* and was ordained on July 6, 1969. He completed a licentiate in sacred theology in 1971 and returned permanently to El Salvador in 1974 before receiving a doctorate the following year for his dissertation, "A Comparison of the Christologies of W. Pannenberg and J. Moltmann."[3] Of Moltmann, Sobrino says, "His book, *The Crucified God*, on whom I wrote my doctoral thesis, has been and is still very important [for me]."[4] On the other hand, he adds, "I have not found verification that God is also on the cross so much in theological arguments or texts, or even Scripture, but in reality: in the suffering servant of our world, El Salvador, Haiti, Rwanda, . . . that does not appear anywhere else."

---

2. World Union of Jesuit Alumni, "Society of Jesus' Contemporary History in Cuba," October 22, 2016 (3 rue Jos Keup, L - 1860 Luxembourg - info@wuja.org). http://wuja.org/2016/10/22/sj-history-in-cuba/.

3. Valenti Gómez-Oliver and Josep M. Benítez, eds., *31 jesuítas se confiesan* (Barcelona: Ediciones Península, 2003), 491; and Jon Sobrino, *Curriculum vitae*, personal files of Robert Lassalle-Klein.

4. Jon Sobrino, "A Su Aire," in *31 jesuítas se confiesan*, 484.

Sobrino explains that theological studies in 1960's Europe
pushed the young Jesuit to "demythologize" his faith, provoking
what he calls a "painful" awakening from the "dogmatic slumber" of naive convictions and beliefs carried from his youth.[5]
While "God and faith were no longer evident," however, he
found solace in Ellacuría's self-implicating 1969 observation
that "Karl Rahner carried his doubts about faith with elegance."
Upon returning to El Salvador in 1974, Sobrino says, "I went
through another awakening."[6] Several of the writings in chapter
four, "Spirituality of Liberation: Awakening from the Sleep of
Inhumanity," describe the surprising joy of Sobrino's life-altering
encounter with God in the crucified common people of El Salvador, tempered by a new-found awareness of the cruelty of their
suffering. Thus, while "liberation and crucifixion provide the
basic tension for Christian faith . . . on this continent,"[7] he tells a
young Jesuit that he was surprised to discover that "the cross and
martyrdom refer not only to 'sin,' but also to 'grace.'" Sobrino's
point is that, beyond the simple fact of their irruption into his
consciousness, "The crucified people also appeared in another
even more surprising way as good news, grace, and salvation,
without which I would not have done anything."[8] Here, then, is
the true *locus theologicus* for Sobrino's mature encounter with
God, and the basis for his spiritual writings.

Looking back, he says, "It is not that I now possess him, of
course, or that the tragedy of this world no longer cries out for
a theodicy [a theological explanation of how a good God can
tolerate evil]. But . . . I woke up. So today I would not be true
to myself if I did not mention, always with fear and trembling,
God." Thus, he writes,

---

5. Gómez-Oliver and Benítez, *31 jesuítas se confiesan*, 489.

6. Ibid.

7. Jon Sobrino, *Jesus the Liberator: A Historical-Theological View*
(Maryknoll, NY: Orbis Books, 1993), 1.

8. Ibid., 483–84.

> In addressing the reality of this God I have written that he is the God of life, a defender of the poor and a denouncer of the oppressor, the God of the resurrection who gives hope to the victims and the crucified God who is like them, the *Deus semper maior* and the *Deus semper minor*, the God of the promise who is always before us and mysteriously draws us to him, the Father and Mother God, who welcomes us with forgiveness, compassion, and tenderness. With these words I can only stammer who this God is, God's essence, so to speak.[9]

He concludes, combining Karl Rahner's statement that "God is the holy mystery," with the realism of Porfirio Miranda's observation that "the problem is not finding God, but encountering him where He said he would be . . . in Matthew 25," among the poor and rejected of this world.

MYSTERIUM LIBERATIONIS: GOD'S HISTORICAL SELF-OFFER IN THE CRUCIFIED PEOPLE

> This is the marrow of liberation theology [and spirituality] . . . that the crucified people themselves are bearers of salvation. The one chosen by God to bring salvation is the servant, which increases the scandal. We sincerely believe that theology does not know what to do with this statement.   —Jon Sobrino, *The Principle of Mercy*, 53

Jon Sobrino occupies a unique place as witness and interpreter of the world-altering encounter with God in the crucified people of the planet. The unexpected and joy-filled nature of this experience of God forms the core of Sobrino's spirituality. His spiritual writings are full of memories and stories recounting the "awakening" to the Holy Mystery of God in El Salvador's suffering people of companions like Archbishop Romero, the UCA martyrs, the four North American women assassinated by the Salvadoran National Guard in 1980, and many others.

---

9. Ibid., 489–50.

In response to questions about the genesis of this experience, Sobrino states that, if there is a "before and after" in his life and writings, "I would put the big break at Archbishop Romero."[10] He recalls that on June 19, 1977, the newly ordained archbishop traveled at great risk to celebrate Mass with the traumatized and isolated peasants of Aguilares, El Salvador, three months after the assassination of his friend, Fr. Rutilio Grande, S.J., for his work with impoverished *campesinos*.[11] He says it was Romero who first proclaimed that day, "You are the image of the pierced savior . . . who represent Christ nailed to the cross and pierced by a lance"; you are "the image of all those towns who, like Aguilares, will be broken and defiled."[12] Eight months later, inspired by Romero, Ellacuría recast Moltmann's image of "the crucified God" (on which Sobrino had completed his dissertation three years earlier) as "the crucified people" in a February 1978 essay written for the meeting of the Latin American bishops at Puebla.[13] He describes them as that "vast portion of humankind that is literally and actually crucified by natural . . . historical, and personal oppressions,"[14] and three years later in 1981 he suggests that the crucified people are the "principal" sign of the times "by whose light the others should be discerned and interpreted."[15]

---

10. Jon Sobrino, "Hablando con Jon Sobrino, Hacer Creible la Fe," *Mision Abierta*, Junio, no. 6 (1993): 7.

11. Jon Sobrino, *Archbishop Romero: Memories and Reflections* trans. Robert R. Barr (Maryknoll, NY: Orbis Books, 1990, 2016), 26–27.

12. My translation of Romero's words from Oscar Romero, "Homilía en Aguilares [June 19, 1977]," *La voz de los sin voz: La palabra viva de Monseñor Oscar Arnulfo Romero* (San Salvador: UCA Editores, 1980), 207–12, at 208.

13. This detail is from Jon Sobrino, "El padre Ellacuría sobre Monseñor Romero, ayudas para poner a producir en las iglesias la herencia de Jesús," *Revista Latinoamericana de Teología* 65 (2005): 120.

14. Ignacio Ellacuría, "El pueblo crucificado, ensayo de soteriología histórica," *Escritos teológicos*, II (San Salvador: UCA Editores, 2000), 138.

15. Ignacio Ellacuría, "Discernir *el signo* de los tiempos," *Escritos teológicos*, II, 134.

But what kind of salvation could possibly be said to emerge from the blood-stained history of Latin America's crucified peoples for those who live far away on islands of comfort? Sobrino explains that Archbishop Romero and others have discovered that the crucified people offer two kinds of salvation. First, where God says that the servant will be a "light to the nations" (Isa. 42:6, 49:6), the crucified peoples show the nations of the world "what they really are." That is, the sufferings of the poor majorities of the planet demonstrate to anybody willing to listen that "the solution offered by the First World today is factually wrong, because it is unreal; it is not universalizable. And it is ethically wrong, because it is dehumanizing . . . for them and for the Third World."[16] Second, "the crucified peoples also offer positive salvation."[17] They offer "values that are not offered elsewhere," including "community against individualism, co-operation against selfishness, simplicity against opulence, and openness to transcendence against blatant positivism, so prevalent in . . . the Western world." He synthesizes these in three principles or clues that he describes as gifts "from the victims" of history revealing the true meaning of the resurrection of Jesus for Latin America and the nations of the world.[18]

The Hope of the "Victims"

First, Sobrino believes that the historical *hope of the crucified* in the victory of life over death is the most essential clue "for understanding what happened to Jesus."[19] He argues that "if human beings were not by nature 'beings of hope' or were unable to fulfill this hope over the course of history with its ups and downs, the resurrection texts would . . . be incomprehensible. It would

---

16. Jon Sobrino, *The Principle of Mercy: Taking the Crucified People from the Cross* (Maryknoll, NY: Orbis Books, 1994), 54.

17. Ibid., 55.

18. Jon Sobrino, *Christ the Liberator: A View from the Victims* (Maryknoll, NY: Orbis Books, 2001), 35–36.

19. Ibid., 45.

be like trying to explain colors to a blind person."[20] He says that New Testament accounts of the resurrection of Jesus call for "hope in the power of God over the injustice that produces victims"[21] and over the many forms of crucifixion and death used to defeat the promises of the Reign.

But where in history do we actually find this hope, and how do we make it our own? Sobrino says the answer "is difficult; [for] it requires us to make the hope of victims, and with it their situation, our own."[22] He insists that only by making the historical hope of history's victims into our own hope can "we progress in finding a God who is loving and on the side of the victims, so we can respond to this God with radical love for them." The disciple, then, is confronted with a two-edged sword. On the one hand, adopting the hope of the victims "makes the question of the ultimate fate of these victims more acute," which is uncomfortable. On the other, however, it means both that "we can . . . 'hope' that the executioner will not triumph over them" and that we are being offered the possibility of "a final and fulfilling hope."[23]

A Praxis of Love

Sobrino's second principle or clue is that the hope of the victims in God's victory over death is only truly understood through a *praxis of love* that takes the crucified people down from the cross. This controversial claim reflects Sobrino's conviction that if "the ultimate root of all hope is . . . always love," then "the Kingdom cannot be understood only as what is hoped for . . . but also . . . as what has to be built."[24] Thus, just as love leads Jesus to initiate the Reign and to accept suffering and death on its behalf, so when he appears to his followers "the risen Lord

---

20. Ibid., 36.
21. Ibid., 42.
22. Ibid.
23. Ibid.
24. Ibid.

sends them out to preach, baptize, forgive sins, feed the faithful, and . . . (Matthew 28:19–20; John 20:23; 21:15, 17) . . . like the earthly Jesus, to heal and cast out demons (Mark 16:17–18)."[25] Sobrino's point is that love of neighbor is made real (or historicized) through action on behalf of the beloved.

Sobrino then argues that "understanding today that Jesus has been raised by God entails [not just] the hope that we can be *raised*, but . . . also that we have to be, in some way, *raisers*."[26] Or to put it another way, the principle analogy of the life, death, and resurrection of Jesus is to be found among the crucified people and those who defend them. Sobrino says that, just as in due course God's "justice was done to the crucified Jesus, . . . so the course of action called for is [for us] to take the crucified people down from the cross."[27] Viewed as a way of following Jesus in light of his second principle, Sobrino concludes with the startling claim, "This is action on behalf of the victims, of those crucified in history, that tries in a small way— with of course no hubris—to do what God himself does: to take the victim Jesus down from the cross."[28]

Sobrino's point, then, is that when the disciple responds to the grace-filled call by Jesus Christ to take the crucified people down from the cross, he or she is caught up in what the Greek Fathers called *theosis*, becoming a living sign of God's work in Jesus Christ (including the resurrection). Unfortunately, however, just as Jesus' prophetic praxis leads inevitably to his crucifixion, so "action on behalf of the crucified . . . is also automatically against the executioners and . . . conflictive."[29] Sobrino says this flows from the fact that, on the one hand, "action at the service of the resurrection of the *dead* [and] . . . the *many* . . . should also be social, political, seeking to transform structures, *to raise them up.*" On the other hand, however, such action inevitably brings

---

25. Ibid., 46.
26. Ibid., 47.
27. Ibid., 48.
28. Ibid.
29. Ibid.

persecution and suffering to the disciples of Jesus, transforming them into living signs of his life, death, and resurrection. Thus, the disciple who responds to the call embodied in the historical reality of Jesus to loving action on behalf of the poor is destined to become, analogously, a living sign of how the reign of God brings both joy and suffering, and how the economy of salvation is carried out in the historical reality of Jesus Christ.

Reality as Mystery

The third clue or gift from the victims of history is that "in the final analysis, to know Jesus' resurrection we have to accept that *reality is a mystery* that is being shown to us gratuitously."[30] Sobrino's point is that "if . . . one confesses [the resurrection] . . . as something real, then it is necessary to have . . . faith in God's possibilities for intervening in history."

Sobrino therefore concludes that Christianity is first a religion of *theosis* (becoming like God) and that our encounter with Holy Mystery is historicized in God's self-offer through the crucified people of today. Thus, Sobrino concludes, "On this journey through history, not going outside history but taking flesh and delving deep into history, it can happen that reality gives more of itself, and the conviction can grow (or decrease) that . . . the journey is enveloped in the mystery of the beginning and the end, a mystery that antedates us, from which we come, which moves us to good and leads us to hope for eternal life."[31] In the end, the strength of these claims lies in the fact that they articulate the experience of the Latin American church in living with the option for the poor, and the unexpected grace given by the crucified people to those who love them.

It is not surprising, then, that we should hear the voice of the UCA martyrs in Sobrino's scandalous claim, "This mystery is grace, and the victims of this world, the crucified peoples, can be, and in my view are, the mediation of this grace. [For] the victims

---

30. Ibid., 53.
31. Ibid., 340.

provide the dynamism—the quasi-physical 'shove'—for carrying out the task of journeying that involves taking the crucified peoples down from their cross."[32] Sobrino confesses that for him, "the greatest encouragement comes from those who inspire with their actual lives, those who today resemble Jesus by living and dying as he did" (no matter who they are). These are the people who, like Archbishop Oscar Romero, grasp what is at stake in this hope, take responsibility for it, and take charge of carrying out Jesus' compassionate, loving, and transformative "practice with spirit." At the end of the day, whether through liberation or solidarity, Sobrino concludes, "This is God's journey to this world of victims and martyrs, . . . it is the way to the Father and the way to human beings, [and] above all [it is the way] to the poor and the victims of this world."

AWAKENING FROM THE SLEEP OF INHUMANITY: THE SPIRITUALITY OF LIBERATION

As we have seen, Sobrino occupies a unique role as both witness and interpreter to the unexpected grace that is the crucified people and those who love them. Recently, Maria Clara Bingemer from the Pontifical Catholic University of Rio de Janeiro told me of Jon's shock and sadness as one of the first to see the broken and violated bodies of the four North American women, raped and murdered by members of the Salvadoran National Guard in 1981. Reflecting on these experiences, Sobrino writes, "I have been surrounded by an immense cloud of witnesses that 'have suffered the shedding of blood,' as it says in the Letter to the Hebrews [9:22], and it has fallen to me to live in the midst of it."[33] He says, "They are people . . . who resemble Jesus in the way they live, in their mission, in what they defend and denounce, and in the reasons for which they are persecuted and assassinated. Magnificent people, with limitations of course, who have made the gospel speak like nothing else, and who have

---

32. Ibid.
33. Ibid., 484.

made the depths of God and Jesus real with spontaneity and naturalness, without even a discernment: this is the greater love."[34]

In a similar, perhaps more personal example, Sobrino recalls that when he learned in Thailand that the Salvadoran armed forces had assassinated his friends and companions he told the audience "spontaneously and with total conviction: 'I must give you bad news: they have assassinated my entire community. [But] . . . I must tell you good news [as well]: I have lived with good men, men of compassion, truth, and love.'"[35] This reaction provides the interpretive (or hermeneutical) key to Sobrino's work: "gratitude and appreciation,"[36] tempered by a realistic awareness of the suffering caused by sin and idolatry. Thus, while "liberation and crucifixion provide the basic tension for Christian faith . . . on this continent,"[37] he insists, "the cross and martyrdom refer not only to 'sin,' but also to 'grace,'" adding in the next breath, "This seems to me the most important contribution from the Salvadoran school of theology ([of] Ignacio Ellacuría, Monseñor Romero . . .),"[38] and, he might have added, Jon Sobrino. Stated more humbly and perhaps clearly, Sobrino says, "I have allowed myself to be welcomed by God . . . , in a modest way . . . to be welcomed by the poor of this world, and to help the human family grow. Needless to say Jesus has opened my eyes to all of this."[39]

How, then, do the spiritual writings of Jon Sobrino diverge from many other treatments of spirituality in order to capture the encounter with God discovered in solidarity and friendship with the poor and rejected of our world? I must confess to you that I struggled with these questions and finally concluded that the best place to begin was with Sobrino's reconstruction of the interpretive (or hermeneutical) circle captured in his definition of spirituality

---

34. Ibid., 340.

35. Gómez-Oliver and Benítez, *31 jesuítas se confiesan*, 485.

36. Ibid., 494.

37. Sobrino, *Jesus the Liberator*, 1.

38. Jon Sobrino, S.J., Letter to Hartono Budi, S.J., June 30, 1999, personal files of Robert Lassalle-Klein, 2.

39. Gómez-Oliver and Benítez, *31 jesuítas se confiesan*, 494.

as "the spirit of a subject—an individual or a group—in its relationship with the whole of reality."[40] For Sobrino, "the spirit of a subject" refers to the fundamental relationships, loves, commitments, and self-understandings that shape, set "in motion," and give "direction" to the relationship of the subject to the realities he or she encounters.[41] This reflects Ellacuría's notion that the historical reality of the subject is finally the product of her response to the realities (natural and historical) she encounters and within which she lives. Lest the reader miss the contrast between the jarring historical realism of this approach and the more exclusively subject-centered focus of many Euro-American approaches, he gives two examples of what he believes spirituality is not. First, "spirituality is not something . . . autonomous on the part of the subject; it stands in relationship with reality"; and second, "this relationship is not a regional (restricted) relationship, or a relationship with other spiritual realities only, but [rather] a relationship with the totality of the real."

Here Sobrino echoes Ellacuría's criticism of four habits of mind that he argues "must be overcome" in order to "do justice . . . to the reality of human knowing and . . . Latin American theological thought."[42] First, understanding has a circular structure that compromises the independence of its claims; second, understanding is basically the comprehension and description of the structures of human meaning; third, the "world" and the things that we take for granted as our "horizon" are human structures created for the communication and maintenance of meaning; and fourth, all knowledge, including theological knowledge, is basically a search for meaning.

Ellacuría argues instead that, first and foremost, "human intelligence is not only essentially and permanently sensible,

40. Jon Sobrino, SJ, *Spirituality of Liberation*, trans. Robert R. Barr (Maryknoll, NY: Orbis Books, 1988), 13.

41. Sobrino, *Jesus the Liberator*, 51.

42. Ignacio Ellacuría, "Hacía una fundamentación del método teológico latino-americano." *ECA* 30, nos. 322–23 (August–September 1975), 418.

but it is . . . fundamentally a biological activity,"[43] which means that its activity (including the interpretive circle) never loses its character as an adaptive function even in its most abstract, meaning-centered, or subject-centered expressions. Second, "the formal structure of intelligence . . . is not to understand and grasp meaning, but [rather] to apprehend reality and to confront itself with that reality." Here, Ellacuría develops his famous claim that "confronting oneself with real things as real" comprises (1) grasping what is at stake in reality (*hacerse cargo de la realidad*), (2) assuming responsibility for reality (*cargar con la realidad*), and (3) taking charge of reality (*encargarse de la realidad*).[44] And third, "Human intelligence is not only always historical, but this historicity belongs to the essential structure of intelligence."[45]

Sobrino concludes with a series of questions that he believes spirituality, particularly Latin American spiritualities, must face: "What is the correct relationship between the spirit of the subject and the reality surrounding that subject?" What are "the minimum demands of this relationship?" And what are "the prerequisites for spirituality as such, and thus for any and every concrete spirituality?" He says, "We are looking for prerequisites that, once fulfilled, will become the foundations on which spirituality will be built, if only the spirit of the subject remains faithful to the internal dynamics of these presuppositions."[46]

Sobrino's answer is that "any genuine spirituality will demand" (1) honesty about the real, (2) fidelity to the real, and (3) a certain *correspondence* by which we permit ourselves to be carried along by the *more* of the real."[60] We should notice that honesty, fidelity, and allowing ourselves to be "carried along" by reality are the very virtues that Sobrino believes are required to actualize Ellacuría's three moments of sentient intelligence:

---

43. Ibid.
44. Ignacio Ellacuría, "Hacía una fundamentación del método teológico latinoamericano," *Escritos teológicos, I* (San Salvador: UCA Editores, 2000), 207.
45. Ibid.
46. Ibid., 14.

(1) "grasping what is at stake in reality" requires honesty, (2) "assuming responsibility for reality" requires fidelity, and (3) and "taking charge of reality" requires a willingness to be "carried along" by its possibilities in order to change it.

This description of what a genuine spirituality "will demand" is rooted in Ellacuría's notion that our apprehensions of reality place claims on us that cannot be ignored. He calls this our "bondedness" (*religación*) to reality,[47] which means that when something is actualized as real for us it creates a corresponding demand upon the subject.[48] He says that we are confronted with a whole series of decisions about whether and how to live by the truth of the realities we encounter and receive. At the end of the day, therefore, our fundamental and unavoidable relationship with the "power of the real" presents us with a steady diet of choices regarding whether and how to appropriate our personal spiritual reality in relation to the other realities we encounter.[49]

Here, then, Sobrino has reconstructed the interpretive (or hermeneutical) circle as the interaction between the personal reality of the subject and the natural and historical realities within which he or she lives. In the end, our personal reality is constantly interrupted by our interactions with other aspects of reality. Thus, it is "only by grasping and being grasped by more

---

47. Xavier Zubiri, *El hombre y Dios* (Madrid: Alianza Editorial, 1984), 92–94, 139–40.

48. Ibid., 248.

49. Here, Heidegger's *Dasein* has been replaced by the historical reality of the subject, which gradually emerges and is defined through the stances the human person assumes in her interactions with the natural and historical dimensions of reality. Gadamer's fusion of hermeneutics and praxis has been disrupted by emphasizing the deconstructive dimension of the relationship between the interpreted historical reality of the subject and the reality in which she lives. Ellacuría is critiquing both Heidegger's notion of the hermeneutical circle as the interplay between the subject's self-understanding and her understanding of the world, and Gadamer's claim that hermeneutics is simultaneously ontological and universal in the sense that it underlies all human activities, nothing lies beyond it.

reality" that the human person can become "not just more intelligent, but, finally more real, and more human."[50]

Fair enough, but what is the reality about which Sobrino says Christians must be honest and faithful, and by which we must be "carried along"? It is the historical reality of God's people, the majority of whom are struggling for life on the global margins of islands of wealth and privilege. And what must be the basic stance of followers of Jesus toward this reality? Sobrino says that "the fact that Jesus lived as a good Samaritan" reveals that "the truth about God and human beings is . . . love"[51] and that the universal love of God is perfectly incarnated by love for those universally rejected. For this reason Sobrino changes Anselm's definition of theology as *intellectus fidei* (or faith seeking reason, *fides quaerens intellectum*) to *intellectus amoris* (or love seeking reason, *amare quaerens intellectum*). Properly understood, theology is a spiritual praxis of love for God's people, most especially the rejected, seeking reason. He concludes, "In Latin America we have rediscovered these presuppositions . . . in the practice of liberation. And this . . . has facilitated their rediscovery . . . in the life, practice, and destiny of Jesus."

Sobrino's personal journey reveals the truth of these words. When he returned from studies in at St. Louis University in 1965 to teach at the diocesan seminary and the UCA, he describes his apostolic vision as "helping the people to . . . become a little bit more like Spaniards, Europeans, or North Americans."[52] However, upon returning to El Salvador in 1974, as we saw earlier, Sobrino says "I went through another awakening." But this time the crisis and its impact on his faith were different. He recalls, "I had to wake up from the slumber of inhumanity and my Central

50. Ignacio Ellacuría, "Aporte de la teología de la liberación a las religiones abrahámicas en la superación del individualismo y del positivismo." *Revista Latinoamericana de Teología* 10 (1987): 430.

51. Sobrino, *Jesus the Liberator*, 75.

52. Interview with Jon Sobrino, S.J., by Robert Lassalle-Klein, July 5, 1994, 2.

American Jesuit companions helped me."[53] What is important here is Sobrino's surprising observation that "in this waking up to the reality of the poor, God reappeared—in a new way." "The crucified people 'appeared to me,' *opthe*, . . . as it says in the appearances of the risen Jesus,"[54] and they "appeared in [a] . . . surprising way as good news, grace, and salvation." Here is the true *locus theologicus* for Sobrino's mature encounter with God and interpretive key to his spirituality.

How, then, can we use this key to unlock the spirituality of the martyrs? First, Sobrino says that honesty, fidelity, and correspondence to the encounter with the historical reality of the crucified people became "mediations for our relationship with God."[55] Second, *fidelity* to the crucified people who they had come to know and love was "simply and solely [a matter of] perseverance in our original honesty," even when threatened. He says this fidelity "is exemplified in Jesus," who continues to make the reign of God real in history "though that history now be his cross."[56] Third, honesty with and fidelity to the crucified people turned out to be "our positive response to . . . God's [self-]revelation" in the crucified people,[57] something that he says was not entirely clear at the time. Fortunately, honesty and fidelity *carried them along, drawing* them into "the *for* with which Jesus' life is suffused . . . the *sine qua non* of all future Christian soteriologies . . . [and] the affirmation of what it actually means to be alive . . . [and] attuned to God's creation."[58] Sobrino's argument, then, is that, without fully realizing it, the honesty and fidelity of the UCA martyrs to the crucified people turned out to be their "yes" to God's saving self-offer mediated there.

Here we find the core of the spirituality of the UCA martyrs, which Sobrino insists is also "the marrow of liberation theology.

---

53. Gómez-Oliver and JBenítez, *31 jesuítas se confiesan*, 489.
54. Ibid., 483–84.
55. Sobrino, *Spirituality of Liberation*, 14.
56. Ibid., 18.
57. Ibid., 21.
58. Ibid., 20.

. . . The crucified people themselves are bearers of salvation. The one chosen by God to bring salvation is the servant, which [just] increases the scandal."[59] God has chosen to save the world through the crucified people, or more precisely, through the invitation to accompany the crucified peoples of this world in their struggle for life. The striking historical realism of this spirituality is unmistakable. Christian salvation and spirituality are historicized; honesty, fidelity, and love for the rejected transforms the martyrs to become like Jesus, collaborators with God's saving work in the world and living signs of Jesus' Holy Spirit to a suffering people.

On February 2, 1980, seven weeks before his assassination, Archbishop Romero claimed this spirituality as his own. In words written for him by Sobrino and delivered at the University of Louvain in Belgium, Romero states, "The ancient Christians said, 'Gloria Dei, vivens homo' (the glory of God is the person alive). But I would concretize this by saying: 'Gloria Dei, vivens pauper' (the glory of God is the poor person who lives). For . . . by putting ourselves on the side of the poor and by giving them life we will know the eternal truth of the Gospel."[60]

These, then, are the *marrow* and the *bones* of the spirituality of Oscar Romero, the UCA martyrs, Rutilio Grande, the four North American women, and the faith-filled struggle of thousands of Salvadorans for life. It is a trinitarian spirituality that believes that God acts in historical reality through Jesus' Holy Spirit, transforming the public lives and innermost existences of his followers, making them holy through their "yes" to God's historical self-offer in the crucified people. Sobrino believes this spirituality moves in a salvific and unending spiral of love (or hermeneutical circle) between the personal reality of the disciple and the rejected reality of the oppressed. It is a movement that interrupts their participation in acts of crucifixion, freeing

59. Sobrino, *The Principle of Mercy*, 53.

60. Archbishop Oscar Romero, "Una experiencia eclesial en El Salvador, Centro América," *La voz de los sin voz: La palabra viva de Monseñor Oscar Arnulfo Romero* (San Salvador: UCA Editores, 1980, 1996), 193.

both from dehumanizing roles in a cruel story of oppressor and oppressed, legitimated by closed and systemically distorted circles of communication and interpretation. In this way Sobrino explains, the honesty, fidelity, and love of Archbishop Romero, the UCA martyrs, the American women, and Dean Brackley opened them to the lived reality of the crucified people of El Salvador, transforming them into living signs of the resurrection and the universal love of God for all people.

SUMMARY OF THE CONTENTS

Chapter 1 of the book explores Sobrino's answer to the question, "Who are you?" Most of the material in this chapter is taken from two interviews. The first took place in November 1992 on the third anniversary of the UCA martyrs in the garden of the Archbishop Romero Pastoral Center, and the second was published in 2004 as part of an international series of interviews with thirty-one prominent Jesuits.[61] Through these and other materials, Sobrino provides a narrative frame for his journey, in which he describes "awakening from the sleep of inhumanity" upon his 1974 return from doctoral studies to El Salvador and embracing Medellín's 1968 "preferential option for the poor."

Chapter 2 reveals the gracious God who "appears" as Sobrino "confronts" the reality of El Salvador and his place in it. We hear about theologians from Europe whose ideas helped him, Karl Rahner and Jürgen Moltmann, but it soon becomes clear that he considers reality his most important teacher, and that "the most real reality . . . is the life and death of the poor . . ., a reality that forced me to look at everything else from its standpoint."[62] And we hear how Archbishop Romero, Ellacuría, and the four North American women, help open his mind and heart to the crucified people, in whom he discovers the Mystery of God.

---

61. Sobrino, "A Su Aire," in *31 jesuítas se confiesan*, 483–500.
62. Jon Sobrino, *Companions of Jesus: The Jesuit Martyrs of El Salvador*, ed. Ignacio Ellacuría et al. (Maryknoll, NY: Orbis Books), 6.

Chapter 3 then turns to the crucified people themselves as the historical continuation of God's self-offer in Jesus, and as the way to Christ. Sobrino simply says, "I have done nothing more than—starting from Jesus—to elevate the reality we are living to the level of a theological concept."[63] He explains why he believes that "Christ has appeared again in Latin America," the importance of what he calls "the reality principle" for spirituality, and his reflections on the "psychological impact" of the deaths of his friends and companions.

Chapter 4 explores the surprising sense of gratitude and appreciation that arises from his encounter with God in the suffering people of El Salvador, tempered by a realistic awareness of the role of sin and idolatry in their crucifixion. We see Sobrino challenging aspects of spirituality as it is conceived of by certain writers in Europe and the United States grounded in his convictions that the personal and spiritual dimensions of the subject are shaped by her response to the realities within which she lives. And he explains how he came "to discover that reality was full of joy," which he largely credits to the examples of Archbishop Romero and the crucified "common people" of El Salvador.

Finally, the volume ends with Sobrino's "Letter to Ellacuría," in which he welcomes Fr. Dean Brackley, S.J., a US Jesuit, onto the holy ground of those who have given their lives in love and joy to the crucified people of El Salvador. Sobrino's profound appreciation and reverence for Dean's deeply felt love for El Salvador's common people shows us that he treasures this kind of love above all, more than nationality and politics.

The volume includes an appendix with two entries. First is "Jon Sobrino's Translation of Ellacuría's Three Moments of "Facing Up to Real Things as Real." Early attempts to translate these phrases into English have been questioned by Sobrino and

---

63. Jon Sobrino, *Jesucristo liberador. Lectura histórica de Jesús de Nazaret*, trans. Paul Burns and Francis McDonagh, Francis (San Salvador: UCA Editores, 1991), 30, my translation. See Sobrino, *Jesus the Liberator*, 8.

scholars at the UCA, which should not be considered surprising, given that they involve a difficult wordplay in Spanish. In 2009, as editor for a special edition of *Theological Studies* on *The Galilean Jesus*,[64] I asked Sobrino to clarify his preferred translation for the three phrases, which appeared in the Spanish version of his article. The entry includes Sobrino's preferred translation as well as a short transcript of our exchange.

The second entry in the appendix documents is Sobrino's "Letter to Fr. Kolvenbach, S.J., Explaining Nonadherence to Notification from the Congregation for the Doctrine of the Faith." This copy of the letter was personally delivered to me by Fr. Sobrino, and, as far as I know, it is the first and only version of this letter to be published under his name. Thus, it is important as a historical document and as a reflection of Sobrino's position regarding the 2006 criticisms of the CDF.

The volume concludes with a list of the works cited in the various texts.

---

64. Robert Lassalle-Klein, with Elizondo, Virgilio, and Gutiérrez, Gustavo, eds. *The Galilean Jesus*. Special Issue of *Theological Studies* 70, no. 2 (Spring 2009).

1

Who Are You?

In this chapter, we discover Jon Sobrino's answer to the question, "Who are you?" Sobrino was sent as a nineteen-year-old to El Salvador from Spain in October 1957, a second-year seminarian under the wise direction of Fr. Miguel Elizondo, S.J., director of the new Jesuit novitiate in El Salvador. Elizondo and Ignacio Ellacuría would later lead the Christmas 1969 retreat at which the Central America Jesuits embraced God's preferential option for the poor discerned by the Latin American bishops a year earlier in Medellín, Colombia.[1] We relive Sobrino's 1974 return to El Salvador from doctoral studies at the Hoch Schule Sankt Georgen in Frankfurt, Germany, and his painful "awakening from the sleep of inhumanity." Ellacuría would become his closest collaborator and friend in the Central American University (UCA) community, accompanying the young Jesuit as, Sobrino says, El Salvador's "crucified people 'appeared to me,' opthe as it says in the apparitions of the risen Jesus, they allowed themselves to be seen."

In interviews and personal reflections, we hear Sobrino's stories of "magnificent people . . . who have made the gospel speak like nothing else, and who have made the depths of God and Jesus real with spontaneity and naturalness." We hear his

---

1. The full story of this journey is told in Robert Lassalle-Klein, *Blood and Ink: Ignacio Ellacuría, Jon Sobrino, and the Jesuit Martyrs of the University of Central America.*

bittersweet conclusion, "I have been surrounded by an immense cloud of witnesses that 'have suffered the shedding of blood,' as it says in the Letter to the Hebrews [9:22], and it has fallen to me to live in the midst of it." And we nod in agreement as he replies to Rahner's statement at the end of his life that "I would have liked to have loved people more," stating, "Me too. I would like to have more love for all the men and women who suffer so cruelly, in the Third World . . ., but also in other worlds, AIDS patients, drug addicts, broken families, young people without a future, helpless old people." In these and many other places, the portrait of a kind and gentle spirit emerges who writes, "When I do not have much to say to God, the prayer of Saint Francis of Assisi comes to my mind: 'Lord, make me an instrument of Your peace.'"

And yet, the world of poverty and revolution in which he lives is anything but peaceful, which provokes deeper questions. The reader wonders, for instance, what Sobrino means when he says, "Being real—not just authentic or perfect . . . —or being unreal, has become a fundamental problem for me." But we better understand his dilemma when he explains that the common people "are always there asking me, who I am, what I do, for whom do I live and work. In more abstract terms, they ask me if I am 'real' in this world of theirs, or if I am 'unreal,' a kind of exception or anecdote on the planet they call Earth." And we accompany him down the road of "becoming real," as he confronts the realities of idols and death, the limits and possibilities of contemporary Catholic theology, and the importance for common people of idealistic dreams and visions in the face of society's cynicism and hopelessness.

The very personal reflections in this chapter help us to understand how, for Sobrino, "the problem is not finding God, but encountering him where He said he would be" in the crucified people. We experience his surprise at the joy that he finds there. For example, in recalling the discovery of Archbishop Romero that "with this people it is not hard to be a good shepherd," he reveals his own unexpected revelation that "there is something in them that produces peace, hope, joy." We feel his humble grat-itude when, moments after learning of the murders of his closest friends and Jesuit companions he says, "I must give you bad news: they have assassinated my entire community. And I must tell you good news [as well]: I have lived with good men, men of compassion, truth, and love." We appreciate the maturity of his statement on the third anniversary of their deaths: "I feel joy because I had the privilege of seeing in them people, not saintly and perfect in the conventional sense, but normal people with a very clear direction in their lives." And we respect the humanity of his self-understanding that "God has come to meet me in a call that I used to name 'a vocation to religious life,' and which I now experience as a 'larger vocation' . . . of helping—together with others—to humanize this creation of God."

Most of the material in this chapter is taken from two inter-views, which offer uniquely personal glimpses into Sobrino's heart and mind shortly after the assassinations and fifteen years later. The first took place in November 1992 on the third anni-versary of the UCA martyrs in the garden of the Archbishop Romero Pastoral Center, where most of them died. The second was published in 2004 as part of an international series of inter-views with thirty-one prominent Jesuits. All texts in this section are translated from Spanish originals by Robert Lassalle-Klein.

"IF SOMEONE WANTS TO KNOW [WHO I AM], . . . BETTER TO ASK THE CRUCIFIED PEOPLE"

You ask, "Who are you?" Thinking a little—and I hope without falling into cheap demagoguery—, what comes to me is that, if someone wants to know, and if I myself want to know, it would be better to ask the crucified people. They know who we are, who I am—an answer that is not far from another traditional reply: God knows us better than we know ourselves.

Since you ask, however, maybe I can say something more about "who I am." In January 1990, I think it was Tuesday the twenty-second, I appeared on Spanish Television with Mercedes

Mila on her program. It had been two months since they murdered the Jesuits, my companions, and the program was obviously laudatory of them and, by extension, of the surviving
Salvadoran Jesuits. In this context, the last question-comment
that Mercedes stated was: "Jon, you in El Salvador are made of
sterner stuff." I answered without thinking: "I do not know what
stuff we are made of, but whatever it is, the Salvadoran people
have done it to us." The answer is romantic, but I hope it is not
far from the truth.

Who would I like to be? I would like to be a person who is
"honest about reality," an idea that I have developed theoretically several times. I would like to be a human being and a
believer who is affected by reality, and, professionally, one who
theologizes about realities. I understand all this according to the
visionary words of Ignacio Ellacuría: grasping what is at stake in
reality by being active in it; carrying reality by assuming responsibility for it; and taking charge of reality, including its burden.
Lacking this reference to reality; faith, the Church, the Society
of Jesus, theology, culture, art . . . are becoming increasingly
senseless for me, though that may also be due to a limitation of
mine. In a phrase that I added to the aforementioned three of
Ellacuría, I would also like [to say] *being carried* by reality, that
reality picks me up and carries me: whether it be [through] real
faith, real hope, real love, the real suffering of this world, of the
poor, of the martyrs, [and/or] those who pick up and carry me
and my faith. It is grace.

This little "obsession" with reality has led me to emphasize
the need, first of all, to not conceal or manipulate reality, to not
violate the eighth commandment that says, "Do not lie." It's also
[true] that reality is, in good part, a scandal, and that there is a
transcendental relationship between scandal and concealment.
Where there is scandal, there is, by necessity, concealment, and
the magnitude of the cover-up corresponds to the magnitude of
the scandal. Therefore, we must comply with the eighth commandment: to unmask the cover-up. In that sense, I would like
to be "honest about reality." By doing that we do not yet become

prophets, but at least we become human. In this sense, I am concerned that, in the Church and the Society of Jesus, silence is often requested, especially in the face of actions by the hierarchy, by virtue of some principle or way of proceeding that relativizes or makes the word of truth, denunciation, or honesty about reality of secondary importance.

I would also like to be generous in a world that is cruel for the majorities. In the aforementioned program with Mercedes Mila, when asked about "my" right to life, about not risking it in El Salvador, my spontaneous response was that "I do not have rights, the people have them." Hopefully this is true, at least a bit. I must say that, when I have had problems with the Vatican, they have not affected me much personally, and not because of my great virtue or disdain for the hierarchy, but because they appear small when compared to the treatment that the poor receive from the powerful.

Finally, and at the end of the day, I would like to "do good," simple as that. When I do not have much to say to God, the prayer of Saint Francis of Assisi comes to my mind: "Lord, make me an instrument of Your peace." And, without falling into mystification, I add: "And even if I am not the instrument, may there be peace, life, dignity, justice and hope in this world. "

—"A Su Aire," 486–88

"WHAT DO YOU FEEL NOW?"

Interviewer: They massacred six Jesuits from your community right here, as well as Elba and her daughter Celina. What do you feel now, three years later?

Sobrino: Three years after the assassinations, I am reminded of the cruelty that exists in this world of ours. It is a terrible thing . . . which continues, for example, in Guatemala. I just read a good summary of the book by Ricardo Falla, *Massacres in Guatemala*, hundreds of indigenous people massacred . . . Yet, paradoxically, we live in a world that wants to ignore these things

. . . When I think about the Martyrs after three years, I feel great joy. I say this sincerely, three years later I feel more joy than anything else.

Interviewer: Why this joy?

Sobrino: I feel joy because I had the privilege of seeing in them people, not saintly and perfect in the conventional sense, but normal people with a very clear direction in their lives. Each person's life consists in the love that we have placed in others. This is so fundamental; and it is what fills me with joy when I remember them. That is why what most inspires me is to see the people who, here and everywhere, remember them with true affection. A lot of people come through here. There are thousands of people who enter this building, go out to the garden, look, pray, speak with Obdulio [widower and father of the two women assassinated with the Jesuits]; for some, their eyes moisten . . . My perception is that they all leave better than when they entered. There is something holy and sanctifying in this place. Perhaps the roses now symbolize more love than tragedy . . . I usually say, what I would like to do is to be a custodian of holy places, the custodian of this garden . . .

To put it another way: having witnessed that in this world it is still possible to be human and a believer—because there has been a lot of love—; that really moves me. This is, in the end, what I feel after three years.

Interviewer: We have already celebrated the third anniversary and are beginning the fourth year. These things that you feel, how do they influence your life and your work as you face the future?

Sobrino: For the future, one thing is very clear. I'll say it in a few words. Whatever course the country follows, from these people and so many others, from Archbishop Romero and of course, from Jesus of Nazareth, we must keep walking toward the light of making this world more human, more fraternal, with more justice, and more tenderness. I would feel like a great traitor if I said, "Good, it's fine; we have done enough." No. The love built up over time, pushes us to keep going forward.

—"Hablando con Jon Sobrino, Hacer Creible la Fe," 6–7

"BEING REAL HAS BECOME A FUNDAMENTAL PROBLEM FOR ME"

My everyday world for many years has been El Salvador, its men and women, children and the elderly. Their life is very hard. Years of repression and war have passed, and many more years of poverty, injustice and oppression. In the face of obstacles and impassable ravines, they hold on to hope, whose secret they only know. As for me, they are always there asking me, who I am, what I do, for whom do I live and work. In more abstract terms, they ask me if I am "real" in this world of theirs, or if I am "unreal," a kind of exception or anecdote on the planet they call Earth.

Being real—not just authentic or perfect . . .—or being unreal, has become a fundamental problem for me, and for a long time my greatest fear has been that of being unreal, a fear that does not disappear because I belong to a Christian church or to the Society of Jesus. . . . They ask me, in short, if I live in what I usually call ecclesiastical, social and human "docetism," that is, in a realm of reality created by myself, so that I do not have to live in real reality, words that, though they sound redundant, are not. In this sense, my everyday world—the world of the poor, the crucified people as Ellacuría and Archbishop Romero used to say—is first and foremost a brief interruption. Without knowing it, the poor are prophets, even though they have been benevolent with me I believe, perhaps because they associate me with others with whom I have lived and worked, including Rutilio Grande, Archbishop Romero, and Ignacio Ellacuría.

—"A Su Aire," 483

"IN 1974 THE CRUCIFIED PEOPLE *APPEARED* TO ME"

When I first came to El Salvador in 1957 I did not see things this way. But when I finally returned in 1974, like many others, this crucified people "appeared to me," *opthe* as it says in the apparitions of the risen Jesus, they allowed themselves to be seen. I have already said that the first thing was being seen as a brief interruption, but the crucified people also appeared in a more surprising way without my having done anything, as good news, grace and salvation. Ignacio Ellacuría sensed and articulated very well—in a pioneering manner—the salvific, welcoming, gospel-inspired potential of the crucified people. And he said that the deepest root for understanding them is as the suffering servant of Yahweh today, the one chosen by God to bring light and salvation to the nations. God is present in the servant, hidden, but finally God.

[Jürgen] Moltmann will understand what I am saying very well. His book, *The Crucified God*, on whom I wrote my doctoral thesis, has been and is still very important [for me]. However, I have not found verification that God is also on the cross so much in theological arguments or texts, or even Scripture, but in reality: in the suffering servant of our world, El Salvador, Haiti, Rwanda, there is an ultimacy, of demand and of invitation, of judgment and of welcome, that does not appear anywhere else. In the words of Saint Ignatius, "divinity hides in the Passion [of Jesus]," but it is there.

This people is not just a crucified people. In them is also found—said with simplicity and without demagoguery—resurrection. It is there in their great hopes, in the limitless freedom and love they have recently shown in many places; although, like everything that belongs to the people, the world wants to forget it and bury it as part of the tragedy of our world that produces these crucified peoples. And there is also resurrection in a thousand small gestures, as magisterially articulated by Pedro Casaldaliga, Benjamin Gonzalez Buelta, and Dolores

Aleixandre. Archbishop Romero said, without being disingenu-
ous and informed by a lucidity filled with love: "With this people it is not hard to be a good shepherd." There is something in
them that produces peace, hope, joy.

This environment has been concretized for me in a history of
persecution and martyrdom in the country, in the Church, in the
Society of Jesus, in the University [of Central America], and in
my community. The quantitative data is impressive: for the last
twenty-five years I have been surrounded by an immense cloud
of witnesses that "have suffered the shedding of blood," as it
says in the Letter to the Hebrews [9:22], and it has fallen to me
to live in the midst of it. And, since you ask, with my community
I suffered threats, police inspections, and bombs at home and at
the University . . . And the qualitative data is greater still. They
are people being martyred right now who resemble Jesus in the
way they live, in their mission, in who they defend and what
they denounce, and in the reasons for which they are persecuted
and assassinated. Magnificent people, with limitations of course,
who have made the gospel speak like nothing else, and who have
made the depths of God and Jesus real with spontaneity and naturalness, without even a discernment: this is the greatest love. In
Thailand, where I was visiting when they murdered my brothers
from the UCA, they invited me to say a few words. I answered
spontaneously and with total conviction: "I must give you bad
news: they have assassinated my entire community. And I must
tell you good news [as well]: I have lived with good men, men of
compassion, truth, and love."

They are also passive martyrs, women, old people and innocent children, murdered at that time in El Mozote, like those
being murdered today in Rwanda, lacking even the freedom
to escape death. They are men and women who truly bear the
sin of the world, which has been described in a thousand ways,
although I do not know if the world will someday come to
believe that this barbarity is true. With a certain sense of helplessness, let me once again repeat the words of Teresa de Flo-
rensa, a Catalan religious sister who works in the Great Lakes:

These human beings are humanity's garbage. There are millions of leftover people in our world. No one knows what to do with them, and they are aware that they do not matter to anyone. They carry in their skin an entire history of suffering, humiliation, terror, hunger, and death. Their dignity is wounded [. . .]. But this work with the refugees of the Great Lakes is also an invitation to trust in the human person, in her ability to overcome even the worst conditions. It is a collaboration with a group of people able to reclaim their dignity.

This is, for me, the best environment. As a christologist, the crucified people, always hoping in a resurrection, are the fundamental hermeneutical principle for understanding God and his Christ. As a believer and human being, they are the ones who give encouragement and ultimate direction when I ask myself, with Kant, 'What I can know?', that reality is, despite everything, a promise; that what I have to do against structural sin is to take the crucified peoples down from the cross; that I am allowed to wait; that, against all expectations, justice will be done to the victims; that I can celebrate: In the midst of cruelty and sadness, there is the joy of a humanity in which good, welcoming, human beings also exist.

In the everyday world in which I move, there is a capacity for welcome. And if that world welcomes us—welcomes me—salvation exists. I have no doubt that the grace—an abstract word—, the love, the mercy, the forgiveness, the welcome that goes out to meet others, is real. With this, it is easier for us to overcome hubris and arrogance, to which we are all inclined; to say nothing if we are white, men, priests with authority, educated and hold doctorates . . . With this we can be humanized. And although we can control neither the language nor the idea, perhaps we can say "with intellectual honesty" that underlying reality is goodness, that God is good and that it is good that there is God.   —"A Su Aire," 483–86

THE REALITY OF IDOLS

We have taken the reality of idols very seriously in El Salvador, not only from a subjective perspective: the possibility of making what is not God into an absolute, but rather from the point of view of objectivity: that which we actually make into an absolute. Von Rad showed years ago that, for the prophets of Israel, the idols were first of all historical, rather than religious, realities: the great powers of this world and the accumulation of wealth. Idolatry is, then, to place one's ultimate trust in them. In El Salvador, Archbishop Romero developed the same idea for today from a pastoral perspective, and Ignacio Ellacuría did it from a theological perspective: idols are the absolutization of capital, the absolutization of national security, and the absolutization of grassroots political organizations. Those were the examples of the nineteen-seventies and eighties, although they never really go away. I say this so that one does not think that idolatry is a problem of "primitive" peoples, but that they are, above all, a problem for developed peoples, industrialized democracies. And fundamentally—and moreover the worst aspect of idolatry—is that these present day idols—like the god Moloch—demand victims in order to survive. The one billion five hundred million human beings who live on less than a dollar a day, those are the victims today. I do not have any doubt that idols exist, even though, as I said earlier, they seek to cover themselves up. They seek at a minimum to not look like idols that bring death, but as mere—surmountable—shortcomings of the system.

I have tried in theory and in practice, along with others, to unmask and fight against these idols—which has been a cause of the threats and persecutions that have consequently come upon us. But the "little idols" remain, [including] my own, the ones you are asking about. To put it plainly, when I think of Father Arrupe I see how much simplicity I lack, and how much *hubris* remains in me. When I think of Archbishop Romero, I see how much I lack in closeness to the poor and how much distance remains. When I see people who are poor, I see how much I lack in regards to poverty, or austerity at least, and how many comforts I have. When I think of Jesus, I see how much I lack in compassion, and how much selfishness remains in my life. I have not forgotten one of the last interviews they did with Karl Rahner. They asked him what he would have liked to have done better and he answered: "I would have liked to have loved people more." Me too. I would like to have more love for all the men and women who suffer so cruelly, in the Third World as I have already said, but also in other worlds, AIDS patients, drug addicts, broken families, young people without a future, helpless old people . . .   —"A Su Aire," 488–89

WHO IS GOD?

God? I do not know if anyone can give an answer to the question, "Who is your God?" So I return to what I said before: perhaps the poor have a sense of who is my God?—and, of course, God himself knows—. But perhaps I can add a few things. I had to live in the United States and Germany during the heyday of the masters of suspicion, secularization, the death of God in philosophy, and during the era of demystification in theology. The "awakening from dogmatic slumber" called for by Kant was a true awakening, and it was painful. Little by little, a powerful force was pulling away, like layers of skin, old convictions and beliefs. God, faith, were no longer evident. I remember hearing Ellacuría say in 1969 that "Karl Rahner bears his doubts about faith with elegance," which I think he applied to himself as well.

But in 1974 I went through another awakening, the one that Antonio Montesinos was demanding from the Spanish *encomenderos* [holders of Spanish colonial land grants] in Hispaniola in 1511: "How can you be sunk so deep in unfeeling sleep?" [Bartolomé de las Casas. *Historia de las Indias*, 171–79]. I had to awaken from the sleep of inhumanity, and my fellow Central America Jesuits helped. Also, in this waking up to the reality of the poor, God reappeared—in a new way. It is not that I now possess him, of course, or that the tragedy of this world no longer

cries out for a theodicy [a theological explanation of how a good
God can tolerate evil]. But, with peace and simplicity, and above
all, together with others, I believe I woke up. So today, I would
not be true to myself if I did not mention, always with fear and
trembling, God.

In addressing the reality of this God, I have written that he
is the God of life, a defender of the poor and an accuser of
the oppressor, the God of the resurrection who gives hope to
the victims and the crucified God who becomes like them, the
Deus semper maior and the *Deus semper minor,* the God of
the promise who is always before us and mysteriously draws
us to him, the Father and Mother God, who welcomes us with
forgiveness, compassion, and tenderness. With these words, I
can only stammer who this God is, God's essence, so to speak.
Many years ago, however, I was impressed by what Karl Rahner
said. "God is the holy mystery." Mystery, because God is inef-
fable, and holy because, unlike what is said in religions, God
has come close. And in this same connection, I remember other
words of his: "Catholic theology, in spite of its many dogmas
and ethical norms, says only one thing: the mystery remains forever mystery."

These words continue to impress me to this day, but now I
add others that I read years ago in a book by Porfirio Miranda:
"The problem is not finding God, but encountering him where
He said he would be"—which is the ongoing demand and invitation of Jesus in Matthew 25—. . . And there are also those
of Ellacuría: "With Archbishop Romero God passed through El
Salvador." There are, then, places of God, including the greatest place: Jesus of Nazareth, "the one who went around doing
good," "the good news of God." About this, it has fallen to me
to write a lot, so I am not going to expand on it now. I just want
to say that whatever the scholarship on Jesus, more real than
that is the conviction that God, the deepest aspect of the saving
and blessed dimension of reality, has become present in Jesus . . .
and in so many men and women who have followed his path to
this day.

Stated in more existential terms, I believe that God has come out to meet me in a call, which years ago I spoke about as a "vocation to religious life," and which today I experience as a "greater vocation," the call to humanize—as much as possible—this world. Accordingly, the experience of God would be a remembering (again passing through the heart), a remembering that is not anchored in the past, but rather one that returns to what is fundamental.

God continues to meet us as an attraction and an invitation to walk in history, humbly as Micah says, always practicing justice and loving with tenderness. In doing this, and it not being able to be otherwise, despite obscurities and external difficulties, and despite limitations and internal failings, I believe that God is present. That end, in which God gives himself all in all, has an irresistible power of attraction.

Finally, in a world of lies, inhumanity, and provisional arrangements, God is like the sanctuary of truth, of goodness, of finality. And God is like that personally as well: in him there is welcome and mercy, inspiration and encouragement. "Father" and "Mother" are just words, but they say a lot. Quoting Karl Rahner again, "God has forever broken the symmetry of possibly being salvation and condemnation. God is salvation."

Without this mystery, I think I would not know how to live. It is useless, useless to either explain it or to alleviate it. But, at least for me, this mystery is useful for everything, because it makes us be, walk, get out of ourselves and, thus, find ourselves and others.   —"A Su Aire," 489–90

DEATH

I was very afraid of death in my first years as a Jesuit, and remember how I was struck by the masses for the dead that we attended in the church of Santa Tecla during the novitiate (1957–1958); basically, they scared me. Subsequently, age and circumstances [in El Salvador] have normalized my view of death, if those things can be normalized. Since 1974, my second arrival in El Salvador, death has frequently haunted me, terribly close in the country and my community. I have also received personal threats. But not only have I become accustomed to it, but I have learned to see, I believe, its ambivalence. The negative is clear, especially the eternal question: is this world so cruel that death bizarrely scours the countryside among us, among the poor, [in] El Mozote, Rwanda, East Timor . . .? Can this "metaphysical aberration" be somehow "patched up?" On the other hand, I have also seen that in death there can be love and fulfillment. I have seen it, and that's why I say it. Death is, perhaps, a scandalous and paradoxical way of showing that human beings have lived and go on living. Personally, I anticipate death—whatever my psychological situation—as the moment of total availability to mystery, to the mystery of God. Even so, when I remember the death of Jesus, I cannot help feeling shock upon thinking about what my own death will be like. The words that I usually choose about *the beyond* in Masses for the dead, and that I would like to apply to myself, are the following: "Blessed are those who die in the Lord." I believe that in the end, "God will be all in all."

"A Su Aire," 492

THE UTOPIAN VISIONS OF THE POOR

The neighbor is the "other," a welcome and a question, and above all, the one that makes "us" possible, the one that makes the table shared. About them I would like to say that I am saddened and disappointed that, in the First World, utopian [or idealistic] visions are ignored and even scored as "a thing for uninformed people," a sin of young nations who, for that reason, are forgiven. Sometimes I say with a certain irony, and even a certain combativeness: Europe thinks that it is the measure of all things (what the Greeks said only about the human person), and since utopia has not worked in Europe, it is declared unfounded and foolish, an illusion. But Europe does not include even 10 out of 100 persons in the human family. For many others, however, utopia, *ou*-topia, which does not have a location, is the greatest good, *eu*-topia. I heard Leonardo Boff say he did not want to die without seeing Brazilians eat three times a day. Stated in the form of a thesis, utopia is that the poor might have a just and dignified life, that they would get to speak and have a stool on which to sit at the table . . . And a greater utopia is that the First World, the Western democracies, the world of abundance, might allow itself to be welcomed and forgiven, to be humanized by the poor of this world. I have written several times that human beings are divided into two groups: those of us who take life for granted and those who, what they do not take for granted, is life. For the former it is difficult to believe in utopia. For the others it is easy, [indeed] it is a necessity. Utopia is life.

—"A Su Aire," 492–93

THE CHURCH

The Catholic Church? Hundreds of books have been written about the Church and its present day reality. On the one hand, in terms of honesty about reality, the winds are not favorable as the millennium begins. In addition to the sins committed by men and women belonging to the Church, there are sins that strike more at the essence of Christianity and the life of the Church: the excessive power exercised by the hierarchy, the denial of the ecclesial family as a people of God, the fear that has been lodged precisely in an institutional home of the good news, the denial of human rights in an institution that should be its bulwark, the self-censorship, and the self-deprivation of freedom, all of which do not reflect the freedom of the children of God, but rather the still-operative Eurocentrism . . . As someone said, "the masterpiece of power consists in making itself loved," and many times this is what the hierarchy does, consciously or unconsciously. Sometimes I am wont to think, if I can be ironic, "if it were not for Jesus of Nazareth . . ."

But with equal honesty I must say that this Jesus movement, which has come down to us in the form of the Church, is still real, something that stirs the best in men and women, their hope, their commitment, and continues to shape the Church. Medellin took place thirty years ago, and it seems like as soon as it happened, they wanted to bury it. But its roots were well-planted. We have not wound up choking Medellin, much less the Gospel. Sometimes it looks like a small bit of greenery, but it keeps growing into a leafy tree. The recently deceased Don Helder Camara, Archbishop Romero, Archbishop Gerardi, they are the Church of our time. And together with them, the small Christian communities, solidarity groups that proliferate everywhere, unknown self-sacrificing religious women, like the Salesian women who remained in East Timor when the United Nations delegation and the press envoys left in the face of barbarism and fear for their lives, the martyrs of whom we have already spoken, they are Church.

My model of the current Church, stated provocatively, is to be found back in the Church that began thirty years ago: the Church of Medellin. It was attacked, harassed and almost destroyed—let's not forget—by the powers of this world (armies, economic oligarchies, governments) and in some instances by Church hierarchy . . . But it has not died. Jose Comblin says that it is latent and will resurface at any moment.

For the future, I see, among others, two fundamental problems: one is that, owing to a lack of credibility and "being real," the Church is unable to humanize the countries of abundance. The other problem is the infantilization that is accepted—sometimes even promoted—in order that the Latin American majorities continue, at least, accepting some divine reality. My hope is for a return to Medellin, as I said. Undoubtedly, we must historicize and update this return, but in regards to how to achieve it—perhaps more than discussing how to embody new paradigms—we should [simply] exercise the Church's creativity.

—"A Su Aire," 494–95

CATHOLIC THEOLOGY

What are the most pressing problems for Catholic theology today? There are many: interreligious dialogue, Church ministries, lay men and women (for whom we do not even have a name), a humanized approach to sexuality, the ordination of women, and a long *et cetera*. But, beyond that, the problems are the same as always: God, Jesus of Nazareth, grace and sin, holiness and banality, honesty and *hubris* . . . This would be the place to mention the Spirit, but that always makes me somewhat afraid. In my opinion, rather than talking about the Spirit, theology should speak in the Spirit and with spirit. The most important thing, however, seems to me to be overcoming of what I have called "docetism": that theology does not decide in advance what comprises its sphere of reality, thereby subtly giving in to unreality, which would be a subtle form of gentrification. Zubiri used to say, if I remember correctly, that human beings are the "reality animal." Hopefully, we theologians are such. And one last thought: beyond pluralism—of which I have not ceased to be afraid because it can become an alibi for not doing what needs to be done—hopefully we will do theology together, in solidarity, carrying on one with the other. And hopefully, what engenders this solidarity is not an abstract scholarly ideal, but rather the poor of this world, the crucified Christ.

—"A Su Aire," 496

THE JESUITS AND THE SOCIETY OF JESUS

Regarding the Society of Jesus I would like to say two things. The first is that I am happy with my vocation as a Jesuit. I admire and have affection for many Jesuits, let's call them "people who live simply," who without fuss or much ado dedicate years of their lives, thirty, forty, fifty, to "the care of souls." They are the least known. They may work in parishes, visiting prisons and hospitals, in schools . . . They spend their lives doing good, they pray to God each in their own way and walk humbly with him. Other Jesuits are better known: Karl Rahner, Pedro Arrupe, Ignacio Ellacuría . . . They have been on the frontier, advancing history, suffering attacks from the powers of this world and, sometimes, the Vatican. They are a grace from God. They are the

Ignatiuses, the Favres, the Xaviers of our time. I am happy about two things: that the Society of Jesus continues to produce men who live simply, and men who are visionary, all of them Jesuits who want to serve.

I am also happy that that Ignatius who reflected on God and Jesus, while still a layman, was able to unleash a tradition that has come down to us, above all in his *Spiritual Exercises*. I also appreciate that this tradition has been historicized for our day. I see present day attempts to historicize the *Exercises* in the area of psychology, which in itself can be very healthy, although I will confess at times to some reservations. Here, among us, I believe the most creative work has followed the trajectory of Latin Americanization starting, as Ignacio Ellacuría did, from the poor.

Accordingly, for me, as a Jesuit, but also as a believer and as a human being, the image of the incarnation in the *Spiritual Exercises* is very important: "Seeing a whole world on the road to hell," [we hear] also the words of the three divine persons, "Let us bring about the redemption of the human race." In a world in which the relationship between rich and poor moved from 1 to 30 in 1960, to 1 to 60 in 1991, and 1 to 74 in 1997, the [aforementioned] words of Saint Ignatius continue as a judgment and a demand. The colloquy from the meditation on sin [*Spiritual Exercises*, #53] continues to be decisive: "Before Christ crucified, asking myself, what I have done for Christ, what am I doing for Christ, what am I going to do for Christ?"[2] Ellacuría historicized this in a way that, in my opinion, has not been surpassed: "Before the crucified people, asking myself, what I have done to crucify them, what am I doing to take them down from the cross, what ought I to do in order to raise them up?" To this day, the notion

---

2. It is unclear if Sobrino has intentionally changed the third phrase of the three questions that Ignatius says the retreatant should ask of themselves before the crucified Christ from "what ought I to do for Christ," to "what am I going to do for Christ?" He maintain the Ignatian wording in the reformulation by Ignacio Ellacuría, which follows. See #53, in Joseph Rickaby, S.J., *The Spiritual Exercises of St. Ignatius Loyola, Spanish and English* (London: Burns and Oates, 1915).

of the Two Standards [*Spiritual Exercises*, #136–47, esp. 146, 147] seems brilliant to me: there are two ways of life, two roads that are in conflict, so that the both cannot be accepted. They are the path of poverty and the path of riches. Poverty is against wealth and leads to reproach and contempt, and from there to humility and all good things. That is why Saint Ignatius asked [God] for persecution for the Society of Jesus for following the path of poverty—the path of the poor, which we seek to follow today—, and he strongly warned us against an always-present danger: "Worldly honor and pride." Ellacuría, in an intellectual outburst reminiscent of the Two Standards, offered a "civilization of poverty" as a solution for humanity today.

There is no need to repeat the importance of Jesus of Nazareth for Saint Ignatius. Like Saint Francis of Assisi or Dietrich Bonhoeffer, he is always encouraging us to [develop] an interior knowledge of Jesus in order to love and to follow him. And [when speaking] of God he would tell us that he cannot be controlled, that we must let him be God, not to make him come to where we are, but to go to where he is. And it is also God who fills our lives and our hearts, who makes us blessed. I think that all these things are meta-paradigmatic for Saint Ignatius, as I usually say. They do not change with the passage of time.

In the Society of Jesus, I also see big and little problems. While I believe that everything that I have said above is true, following the 32nd General Congregation in 1975 a new spark has just not appeared, as Father Kolvenbach usually acknowledges. I am worried about the excessive obsequiousness towards the hierarchy and the Holy See, and the exaggerated silence when there are quite enough things to be denounced, with charity of course.

I am also worried about an exaggerated Ignatian fundamentalism and triumphalism: it seems like the Basque of Azpeitia predicted everything or that solutions for everything can be found in him today. To put it another way, Saint Ignatius could be properly considered along with (not only as different from or contrary to) Erasmus, Luther, and Bartolome de Las Casas, for having, with all of them, brought about revolutions and reforms.

In this way, I believe the real contribution of Saint Ignatius would be deepened and we could avoid his absolutization, which can become a personality cult. In addition, I am constantly surprised by the fact that, if something distinguishes the spirituality of Saint Ignatius, it is precisely that, "only God is God."

—"A Su Aire," 496–98

FAVORITE SAYINGS

I remember many aphorisms or, rather, sayings, that have impacted me. I will mention a few: "With Archbishop Romero, God visited El Salvador" (Ignacio Ellacuría). "I am glad, brothers, that our Church is being persecuted. It is a sign that it has been incarnated in the poor. It would be very sad, if in a country where it is being so horribly murdered, there were no murdered priests" (Archbishop Romero). "We must carry out the revolution like someone who has been forgiven" (José Ignacio Gonzalez Faus). "Being a Christian is the simplest thing. The Gospel is a heavy light burden, the more you carry it, the more it carries you" (Karl Rahner). Every once in a while one of those phrases comes out. I am going to recall three, critical ones, which may be why they appeared in the newspapers in a prominent way. "The Church is not afraid of Marxism, it is afraid of God." "Europe lacks mercy." "The money paid to the football player, [Christian] Vieri, is a sin." In regards to other [more] positive sayings, perhaps two will do: "For Jesus, God is a Father in whom he can rest; and the Father is a God who never lets him rest." "God is good and it is good that there is a God."   —"A Su Aire," 499

IS THERE A *BEFORE* AND *AFTER* IN YOUR THEOLOGICAL WORK?

Sobrino: In my theological work, I do not think so. If we have to talk about two stages in my professional life of doing theology, I would put the big break at Archbishop Romero. That is to say, this experience of chilling cruelty that assassinates even people who are close to and beloved by the people for not allowing them to be murdered, this began earlier. When they killed Archbishop

Romero, while Ignacio Ellacuría was still alive, which was very important for my professional life, we began to think together theologically about what he called "the crucified people."

What you say points to something true. Living in a situation of so many crosses, that changes one's way of thinking and doing theology. Among the books that I have written, in the most recent, *Jesus Christ Liberator*, I try to say things that others have said better than me; I quote Rahner, I quote Moltmann, I quote Ellacuría, I quote Boff, of course. But there is a chapter at the end, which I think is not usually present in other christologies, "The Crucified People." This is a different point for theological reflection. In this sense, yes, one can speak of two stages in my theological work.

Interviewer: In the second stage, the presence and function of "reality" has grown a lot in your way of doing theology; isn't that true?

Sobrino: Since you ask me that, I am going to say something that I do not know if I am going to explain it well, and, if it is explained well, if it will be correctly understood; but I would like it to be well understood.

In my life, texts, while being so important, have become less important than reality. And here is the thing to be correctly explained. The Spiritual Exercises of Saint Ignatius—whom I love so much—is a text that I greatly appreciate; but it is a text. And the same can be said of those by Saint Irenaeus, beautiful; or of Saint Paul, which are "inspired" (I am never going to write an "inspired" text). Honestly, I have to say that if I read the first Letter to the Corinthians, a text that impacts me a lot, and I go to *El Mozote*, the reality of *El Mozote*, the real crosses of *El Mozote*, make me understand much better the Paul who was angry with the alienated charismatics. Furthermore, the reality of *El Mozote* does not make me ignore the crucified Christ of whom Paul speaks; quite the contrary.

To put it this way, I see God present, not only in the Word of Scripture (which I believe in through faith, in addition to which one can see how that Word generates life), but also in reality, which I have the privilege of witnessing. Seeing an Archbishop Romero speaking the truth, loving with all his heart, that is much more than reading the life of a saint even though the text is excellent and says that he loved . . . At the theological level, this has enormous consequences, which is that reality also becomes a theological argument. I have also coincided with Ignacio Ellacuría in this regard; in that doing theology is to elevate reality to the level of a concept. And to elevate it correctly and Christianly, undoubtedly we must bear in mind the Magisterium of the Church, the Fathers of the Church, and the Scriptures. But to look at all these texts in themselves without connection with reality, I do not think is doing theology; it is to interpret texts, which is very important. For me, doing theology is to see if God is present in our reality and how he is present. It is tricky. One can make mistakes, and if you are wrong, the blunder causes a stink, right? But if we do not end up saying whether God is present in our reality, what does our theology mean?

In the structure of history, it seems to me, the fundamental theological question is: do we see or we do not see God? That is why the concealment of reality with lies and disinformation is so serious, because it does not allow God to be seen in reality.

There are theologians who know a lot about Saint Augustine, Saint Thomas—and hopefully we will know more, since we have a considerable shortcoming in this area. But if you ask those theologians, "And God, where is God in reality?" many do not respond to that question. Here we know less about the former, but I think we can candidly say, "We have seen the face of God." This is the deepest thing that I see in the things that have happened here and they have changed us.

—"Hablando con Jon Sobrino, Hacer Creible la Fe," 7

WHERE DO WE FIND GOD IN THE REALITY OF OUR WORLD TODAY?

Interviewer: Saying truthfully, "we have seen the face of God" is giving witness to the "Good News," isn't this a form of evangelization?

Sobrino: In its fundamental sense, "evangelizing" is certainly that: communicating "good news" in a way that reality is known, lived, and made better in accordance with the goodness of God, which is present in the human and inhuman reality of our world.

Interviewer: It has been 501 years since the Conquest . . . What "good news" is urgent to announce today?

Sobrino: You call it 501, a year after 500 years. I would like to say something to Spain about that, and it is that I think 501 is going to look a lot like 499. From what I have seen, 1992 has been, basically, lived inadequately (with some exceptions) in Spain. This is because, first of all, the vast majority of Spaniards are interested neither in what America was in 1492, nor in what Latin America is in 1992. Worse yet, the events of 1992 in Spain have been of a type that—an International Exhibition, Olympiads, a cultural capital of Europe—have made us disregard even more what is Latin America. Paradoxically, the attention of the average Spaniard has been diverted, and they have been prevented from knowing more about Latin America because they have been told a lot more about these other things. This is inappropriate. And in the Spain, which is part of Europe where xenophobia is increasing so much, it has again been said, very paradoxically, that today, like five centuries ago, what interests Spain is Spain.

This is the real context. As always, there have been important exceptions. There are solidarity groups in Spain that have wanted to open themselves to the reality of Latin American and to honestly study what happened. This is positive. But, looking at everything together, for example, I think that it has occurred neither to the monarchy nor to the average Spaniard to seriously consider the idea of asking for forgiveness.

Interviewer: How would evangelizing the Church fit into this context?

Sobrino: I don't know. It is not up to me to say. I am not going to create a program. Speaking from Latin America, I will just say one thing. According to Jesus, evangelization is "good news" for the poor. For Paul, the gospel is a crucified gospel (there is wisdom there). For Isaiah, the Servant of God is the gospel or good news of salvation and a light of the nations. And the crucified peoples of today follow that crucified Servant of God. If these crucified peoples are not gospel for Spain or Germany or the United States, then we are mistaken in our understanding what is the gospel.

Interviewer: Given the reality of today's world, where would you advise beginning to seriously consider the question of evangelization?

Sobrino: I would remember, first of all, that "evangelizing" is communicating a "Good News." Which means being very aware that there is bad news and that this must be made known. I say this because I am convinced that the fundamental problem that evangelization has in the countries of the First World is that the reality of bad news is being concealed; and it is being concealed in a way that inhibits the possibility of truly "good news."

I believe that this is the best key to introduce us to truth in evangelization, a mission of the Church that goes far beyond doing catechesis and preaching homilies.

One thing I notice that is missing in this real world in which we live is solidarity. I repeat that there are worthwhile groups, groups that are close to us, people who we love very much. But it is not enough. What solidarity really means is to mutually carry each other; that from over there, they help us here, and as difficult as that is, how much more difficult it is for them to allow themselves to be helped by those [of us] who are here: that they would be open to encountering in these extremely poor countries with so many tragedies, values like community, creativity, generosity, faith and hope, celebration, solidarity, and martyrdom, which I see abounds.

Interviewer: Where do we encounter God in the reality of our world?

Sobrino: It seems to me that in the present environment, especially in the countries of the First World, there are bad experiences because there are bad realities, there are lies and cover ups. I am still surprised—to be honest it leaves me speechless—by the fact that, given all the knowledge they have accumulated in Europe, universities, colleges, schools, the media, abundant television channels, churches, parishes to which people dedicate every Sunday . . . that with all that accumulated capacity for knowledge, they do not end up telling the truth about the world in which we live. An average citizen does not know anything about the human reality of the planet; they don't know how many people die each year from hunger. They breathe in a bad reality, which is ignorance about the human family; not only ignorance, but concealment; and it is not coincidental that this happens.

That first creation, which was good, finds itself deeply vitiated in the First World due to lack of mercy. That there are wounded people by the roadside is clear. There is the growing unemployment in some nations; there are immigrants arriving, some from Africa, others from Latin America; there is the "stranger," a sacred figure of the Old Testament, who was to be received as God himself . . . and there is what drives drugs, etc., etc. There are wounded people by the roadside. And of course, there are millions of wounded people a few miles from Spain, which is geographically close; and Latin America is also very close; now you can get a direct flight to San Salvador and to almost every country; we are getting progressively closer. I do not think the average citizen realizes that there are such wounded people by the roadside, and even less likely, that in response they might configure their lives to heal those wounded people. Of course, none of this makes itself felt in Spanish politics, oriented as it is to living better every day, even if others have to live worse. Nor do I see that universities and colleges, in general, go out of their way to possess and develop forms of knowledge that might help the wounded by the roadside. I think that compassion and mercy are not present and active in Spain.

Interviewer: What does it mean and what does it require of a Church to evangelize in that situation?

Sobrino: I will say it in two ways. The fundamental thing is to introduce truth, mercy and solidarity into the reality in which we live. The fourth conference of Latin American bishops at Santo Domingo in 1992 talked about how to evangelize cultures, especially at the level of cultural experience. But in culture there is something more primary than its concrete expressions, something that is like the air we breathe, that culturally leads us to one side or another, which sensitizes us to some things and desensitizes us to others. I believe that the primary form of evangelization is this evangelization of the cultural environment, introducing truth, compassion, mercy, and solidarity into the air that each and every one of us breathes.

In addition, it seems to me that we must take into account that institutions like the Church and the university are not going to transform the reality of society through media like weapons (because we do not have weapons), or the means of production (we do not have those either), but rather with words: a word that tells the truth, a word that clarifies reality as it is, and a word that stimulates, a word that consoles the disconsolate, a word that inspires the betterment of reality.

Another way of saying this would be that to evangelize is to make a world, in which one not only speaks of God or about Jesus, but where their presence is manifested in reality, creating conditions that allow people to "see" them, and make them credible. I think this is the first and the most necessary step for many people in Spain, after years and years of having made God into a Spaniard and having trivialized him . . . So, I do not know if people still see God as a "mystery," but Church things are not very welcome. It seems to me that a Church that first makes these values felt, and then asserts them, has a better chance of being considered credible. And then, after having made those values present, one can mention without any shame the name of God from Jesus of Nazareth, and the name of that Jesus who is a Christ (this is a "mystery"), and the name of that God from whom Jesus is the Christ.

Interviewer: Are we facing a new opportunity for evangelization?

Sobrino: I do believe in the capacities of Christian institutions for evangelization today. And I believe that now, when it seems to us that it is more difficult to evangelize, is when the Church has a better opportunity to do so. First, because we are at a moment in which few institutions are interested in communicating "good news." They are interested in announcing a more pleasant life, but this is not necessarily good news, because we can have more pleasure and more wealth and be less human. There is a large deficit of "good news" coming from other institutions. The Church has an open field today.

But, in addition to this, and above all, the Church has that mystery of God made present in Jesus, which expresses itself in more truth, more mercy, more solidarity. If we set ourselves to it, we can evangelize today.

—"Hablando con Jon Sobrino, Hacer Creible la Fe," 9

2

God Visited El Salvador

*In this chapter, Sobrino reveals the God who "appeared (*opthe*)" as he "awakened from the sleep of inhumanity" upon returning to El Salvador in 1974. The chapter begins with the Jesuit's, "Letter to Ellacuría," written for the first anniversary of the Central American University (UCA) martyrs. The letter, which would become an annual tradition, provides a unique window into Sobrino's heart and mind. Though widely regarded as perhaps the leading public intellectual of a remarkable group of mid–twentieth-century Spanish Jesuits sent to Latin America, Sobrino tells Ellacuría, "I am convinced that you were a great believer" and that "the fundamental thing you have left me [is] . . . that nothing is more essential than the practice of compassion for a crucified people and that nothing is more human and humanizing than faith." This response captures Sobrino's role as witness to the mysterious presence of God in the lives of El Salvador's poor majorities and the remarkable women and men like Archbishop Romero and the four American women who loved them.*

In what follows, we learn of Ellacuría's appreciation for how his "great teacher, Karl Rahner" handled doubts about God. We discover that, following Sobrino's first encounter with Archbishop Romero on the evening of the murder of Rutilio Grande, "From that night on, . . . Romero's serious, concerned face when I opened the door was like a magnet to me, attracting me to him and overwhelming me with the idea that I must somehow

*help him." We hear that, "personally, I was profoundly struck
. . . by his faith in God, his absolute conviction of God's reality" and that "the God of the poor and the mystery of God are
what Archbishop Romero made present to all who were willing
to listen." We watch Sobrino's spirit fall as he "stood by the
bodies of Maura Clarke, Ita Ford, Dorothy Kazel, and Jean
Donovan," and "felt what I have felt so often since the murder of Rutilio Grande, in 1977." We understand the mixture
of gratitude and anger he experiences before their tragically
shortened lives, which represent "the best the United States
has to offer: faith in Jesus instead of faith in the almighty dollar; love for persons instead of love for an imperialist plan; a
thirst for justice instead of a lust for exploitation." And, we
are perhaps moved by his claim that "with these four Americans, Christ, although he came from a far-off land, was no
stranger in El Salvador."*

*Regarding the Jesuit murders, Sobrino flatly states, "This
time it was different. . . . For days my head was just empty
and my heart frozen." We hear of the phone call in which a
friend explains, "Something terrible has happened." Sobrino
remembers, "My friend read the names slowly and each of them
reverberated like a hammer blow that I received in total helplessness. I was writing them down, hoping that the list would
end after each name. But after each name came another, on to
the end. The whole community, my whole community, had been
murdered, [and] two women . . . with them." Many will identify
with his conclusion: "I felt a real . . . emptiness that nothing
could fill, . . . [and] remembered the biblical passage about the
mothers of the murdered children who wept and could not be
comforted."*

*Yet, Sobrino adds, "I loved my murdered and martyred
brothers very much." He says, "I am very grateful to them for
what they gave me in their lives and for what they have given
me in their death." He explains this is because "in the midst
of cruelty and sadness, there is the joy of a humanity in which
good, welcoming, human beings also exist" and because "now I*

understand a little better what this world's victims mean." This brings us to what Sobrino regards as the central mystery of the God of Israel, the God of Jesus, and the God of the crucified people of El Salvador who "carry the sin of the world, and by carrying it, . . . offer light and salvation to all." We hear the voice of Archbishop Romero, who says, "Interpreters of scripture cannot tell whether Yahweh's Servant proclaimed by Isaiah is the suffering people or Christ who comes to redeem us." And we listen to Ellacuría, who asserts, "This crucified people is the historical continuation of Yahweh's Servant, whom the sin of the . . . powerful of this world continue to strip them of everything, to snatch everything from them, even their lives, especially their lives." But Sobrino himself simply concedes that such claims come from "insight rather than . . . exegetical analysis." And he grants that, while "this theological interpretation of the crucified people as Yahweh's Suffering Servant has taken root in Latin America, . . . in other places it may still seem too bold or simply to be unscholarly pious talk."

We are left, then, with an experience of God in the crucified people that Sobrino unabashedly concedes is a historical product of the "preferential option for the poor" of the church of Central America. And he confronts the reader with the reality that, though it "shows us what we are, we tend to ignore it, cover it up, or distort it, because it simply terrifies us." In other words, it is an experience of God that calls for conversion and change.

In the end, like so much else in his work, Sobrino turns to Archbishop Romero to describe the path from fear to light and grace. He explains that, though "the poor were effectively calling for his conversion, . . . in offering him light and salvation, they also facilitated that conversion—and Archbishop Romero recognized this." Here, then, is Sobrino's version of Rahner's "heavy light burden," which he cites in section one. Sobrino writes, "For me there is no doubt that this is Archbishop Romero's last secret, and I shall reveal that secret. In one of his most felicitous expressions, in words of the kind that cannot be invented, but can only come from the heart, he said, 'With this people, it is not difficult to be a good shepherd.'" The God of the crucified people is a God of love, hope, joy, and community.

LETTER TO IGNACIO ELLACURÍA ON THE FIRST ANNIVERSARY OF HIS DEATH

If asked to sum up in a few words how I remember Ignacio Ellacuría as a human being and a Christian, I could only repeat what I wrote in a letter on the first anniversary of his death.

Dear Ellacu:

For years I have thought about what I would say at the Mass for your martyrdom. As in the case of Archbishop Romero, I never wanted to accept that this would come to pass. But your death was very likely, and the thought of this day has sent me in circles many times. These are the two things that most impressed me about you.

The first is that your intelligence and your creativity had a large impact on me, obviously, yet nonetheless I always thought this was not your most salient characteristic. It is true that these things were very important for you, but you did not orient your life to become a famous intellectual, or a lauded university president. To cite an example, I remember that while you were in exile in Spain you wrote a manuscript that would have made you famous in the world of philosophy. And yet you did not give it much importance, and you did not finish it when you came to El Salvador because you always had other more important things to do: from helping resolve some national problem, to attending to the personal problems of someone who asked for your help. The conclusion for me is very clear: service was more important to you than the cultivation of your intelligence and the recognition that it could bring you.

But whom to serve and why? You served at the UCA, but you did not finally serve the UCA itself. You served in the church, but you did not finally serve the church itself. You served in the Society of Jesus, but you did not finally serve the Society of Jesus itself. The more I got to know you, the more I became convinced that you served the poor of this country, and of all the Third World, and that this service is what gave finality to your life.

You were a faithful disciple of Zubiri, a liberation philosopher and theologian, and a theorist regarding community-based political movements, but you did not fight for those theories as if they were "dogmas." Rather, you changed your points of view, you the inflexible one. And when you would do that, it was always one thing that made you change your mind: the tragedy of the poor. That is why I believe that if you had any fixed "dogma," it was only this: the pain of the crucified peoples.

This brought me to the conclusion that first and foremost you were a man of compassion and mercy, and that what was deepest in you, your guts and your heart, was moved by the immense pain of this people. This never left you in peace. It drove your creativity and your service. And your life, then, was not only service. Rather, it was the specific service of "taking crucified peoples down from the cross," very much your words, the kind of words that are invented not only with great intelligence, but with an intelligence moved by compassion.

This is the first thing I wanted to mention. The second thing I remember about you, and this is very personal, is your faith in God. I will explain what I mean. Faith in God was not made easy by your contact with modern philosophers, most of them nonbelievers, with the exception of your beloved Xavier Zubiri; or the atmosphere of secularization including even the death of God that predominated in the era when you achieved intellectual maturity; or your own critical and honest intelligence, not at all given to easy belief; or finally the great question about God posed by the unjust poverty of Latin America. I remember one day in 1969 you told me something I never forgot: that your great teacher Karl Rahner bore his doubts with great elegance. This brought you to say that faith was not something obvious for you either, but rather a victory.

Yet, nonetheless, I am convinced that you were a great believer, and to me, you certainly communicated faith. You did it one day in 1983 when, upon returning from your second exile in Spain, you spoke to us at the mass of the "Heavenly Father." And I thought to myself that if Ellacu, the thinker, the critic, the honest intellectual, used those words, then it was not just sentimentalism. If you spoke of the Heavenly Father, it was because you believed in him. You communicated faith to me many other times when you spoke or wrote of Archbishop Romero and his God, and when you spoke simply of the religiosity of the poor. And you communicated it to me through your way of speaking and writing about Jesus of Nazareth. In your writings you express your faith that what we human beings truly are has been revealed in Jesus. But there you also gratefully express your faith that Jesus displayed that "more" that surrounds everyone, that ultimate mystery and utopia, which attracts everything to itself. I don't know how much you struggled with God, like Jacob, Job, and Jesus. But I believe that God won you over, and that the Father of Jesus oriented what was deepest in your life.

Ellacu, this is what you have left us, for me at least. Your exceptional abilities can dazzle, and your limitations and defects can leave one in the dark. I believe, Ellacu, that neither has the one dazzled, nor the other obscured, the fundamental thing you have left me: that nothing is more essential than the practice of compassion for a crucified people, and that nothing is more human and humanizing than faith.

These things have come to mind over these years. Today one year after your martyrdom, I say them with pain and with joy, but above all with gratitude. Thank you, Ellacu, for your compassion and your faith.

—"Ignacio Ellacuría, the Human Being and the Christian," 57–60; translated by Robert Lassalle-Klein

MY FIRST ENCOUNTER WITH ARCHBISHOP ROMERO

The Death of Rutilio Grande

My first personal encounter with Archbishop Oscar Romero took place on March 12, 1977. On the afternoon of that day, Father Rutilio Grande, S.J., and two *campesinos,* a boy and an old man, had been murdered near El Paisnal. A few hours later, in the Jesuit house at Aguilares, a large number of persons had gathered—we Jesuits, other priests, sisters, and hundreds of *campesinos,* all had come to weep for the two murdered *campesinos* and for Rutilio, the priest who had proclaimed to us the good news of the gospel.

We had been awaiting the arrival of Archbishop Romero, installed as head of the Archdiocese of San Salvador less than three weeks before, on February 22, and of his auxiliary, Bishop Rivera. The bishops would lead our concelebration of the first Eucharist in the presence of the remains of the three murder victims. But it was growing late, and the prelates had not yet arrived. The people were beginning to show a certain impatience and uneasiness, especially now that night was falling. So Father Jerez, provincial of the Jesuits of Central America, decided to begin the celebration of the Eucharist without them; and all except myself—I no longer remember why—began to move toward the church, which was attached to the house. Suddenly there was a knock at the door. I went to the door, opened it, and there stood Archbishop Romero and Bishop Rivera. The archbishop looked very serious and concerned. I greeted our visitors, and without another word led them to the church. . . .

Uppermost on our minds that night, then, was the dead body of Rutilio, but I was also mightily struck by the serious, preoccupied face of Archbishop Romero. Here was an ecclesiastic of whom I had heard only that he was very conservative and not really very courageous. Here he was, beginning his archiepiscopal ministry not amid a series of solemn celebrations but awash in arrests, torture, the expulsion of priests, and now, suddenly, the blood of Rutilio Grande, one of the priests with whom he had been on the most familiar terms. Who could have foretold that the growing repression of *campesinos* and laborers, which the Salvadoran bishops, at the insistence of Bishop Rivera in particular, had so courageously denounced in their message of March 5, would so quickly come to this?

From that night on, my mental image of Archbishop Romero's serious, concerned face when I opened the door was like a magnet to me, attracting me to him and overwhelming me with the idea that I must somehow help him. Actually, the preconception we had had of him had already been somewhat modified in the course of the clergy meetings of the closing days of February, where he was introduced as our new archbishop; at that time he had asked our help in the serious difficulties he was sure to encounter. My decision to try to help him was an enthusiastic one, then, and it was shared by many. It was also something we all perceived as a matter of urgency, since we all expected things to get very difficult in the immediate future, and we knew that we would do much better if we faced them united as a church rather than in a state of separation and division. And so there had already been a noticeable change in the relationship between Archbishop Romero and ourselves. But that night of March 12 sealed that relationship.

To tell the truth, the change was a surprising one. For one thing, my little contact with him had been rather tense since I had returned to El Salvador in 1974, and the one thing I knew for certain about Archbishop Romero was that he had been a very conservative auxiliary, much under the influence of Opus Dei and an adversary of priests and bishops who had accepted the Medellin line; sometimes he had gone so far as accusing these bishops and priests of "false ideology." He also regarded several Salvadoran Jesuits as "Marxist" and "politicized," and these were precisely the persons under whose guidance I was taking my first steps as a Jesuit and theologian after a seven-year absence from the country. . . .

A Humble Bishop Was Practically Begging Us to Help Him

. . . After Mass, Archbishop Romero asked us priests and sisters to remain in the church. Some of the *campesinos* stayed too, and naturally we made no discrimination. We held a planning session

right then and there, in the late hours of the night, without waiting for the next day or a night's rest. Archbishop Romero was
visibly agitated. He seemed to be laboring under the responsibility of having to do something and not knowing exactly what
to do. After all, the problem facing him was unheard of, and the
question he asked us was elementary. What should we and could
we do, as church, about Rutilio's murder?

Agitated and perturbed, he was nevertheless ready to do
whatever would be necessary, and I could see this. He must have
been afraid, however. The hour had come in which he would
have to face up to the powerful—the oligarchy and the government. I shall never forget how totally sincere he was in asking
for our help—how his words came from the heart. An archbishop was actually asking us to help him—persons whom a
few weeks before he had regarded as suspect, as Marxist! This
gesture of dialogue and humility made me very happy. I reflected
that, while the tragedy of that day seemed such an inauspicious
beginning for Archbishop Romero in his new, archiepiscopal
responsibility, actually it could be a most auspicious one. The
seed of a united, determined, and clear-sighted church, a church
that would one day grow to be so great, had been sown. I felt
great tenderness for that humble bishop, who was asking us,
practically begging us, to help him bear the burden that heaven
had imposed on him, a far heavier burden than his shoulders, or
anyone else's, could ever have borne alone.

I also felt, or seemed to surmise, that something very profound was transpiring deep within Archbishop Romero. Surely
he was uneasy. But in the midst of his uneasiness in those first
moments, with all of his hesitancy about what to do, I think
he was forming the high resolve to react in whatever way God
might ask: he was making an authentic option for the poor,
who had been represented, a scant hour before, by hundreds of
campesinos gathered about three corpses, helpless in the face of
the repression they had already suffered and knowing full well
that there was more to come. I do not know whether I am correctly interpreting what was actually transpiring in Archbishop

Romero's heart at these moments, but I believe he must have felt that those *campesinos* had made an option for him—that they were asking him to defend them. His response was to make an option for the *campesinos*—*to* be converted and transformed into their defender, to become the voice of the voiceless. I believe that Archbishop Romero's definitive conversion began that night. . . .

What was the cause of Archbishop Romero's conversion? I have been asked this question countless times. I have no "objective," psychological answer, nor did I ever speak of this with him personally. . . . Still I should like to set forth my own view of Archbishop Romero's conversion, be it only to show that the interior change of which I speak actually did take place, and that his external behavior is not to be ascribed to any sort of "manipulation."

I believe that the murder of Rutilio Grande was the occasion of the conversion of Archbishop Romero—as well as being for him a source of light and courage to follow his new paths. Archbishop Romero had known Rutilio and had held him in such high regard that he invited him to serve as master of ceremonies at his episcopal consecration. He did not, however, approve of Rutilio's pastoral ministry at Aguilares. It seemed too political to him, too "horizontal," foreign to the church's basic mission and dangerously close to revolutionary ideas. Rutilio had been a problem for Archbishop Romero, then. In fact he was an enigma. Here was a virtuous, zealous, deeply believing priest. Yet this admirable priest's approach to pastoral ministry was one that, at least in Archbishop Romero's eyes, was simply incorrect and mistaken. It was this enigma, I think, that was solved the day Rutilio died. I think that, as Archbishop Romero stood gazing at the mortal remains of Rutilio Grande, the scales fell from his eyes. Rutilio had been right! The kind of pastoral activity, the kind of church, the kind of faith he had advocated had been the right kind after all. Then, on an even deeper level: if Rutilio had died as Jesus died, if he had shown that greatest of all love, the love required to lay down one's very life for others—was this not because his life and mission had been like the life and mission of Jesus? Far from being a deluded, misled follower of Jesus, Rutilio must have been an exemplary one! Ah, then it had not been Rutilio, but Oscar who had been mistaken! It had not been Rutilio who ought to have changed, but himself, Oscar Romero. . . . Of course, Rutilio had been a simple missionary priest, not archbishop of San Salvador, and could not have given examples of the concrete expressions of this new fundamental direction that would be appropriate for the archbishop of San Salvador. It was up to Oscar Romero to find these concrete expressions himself, in function of his particular, critical historical circumstances. Archbishop Romero's conversion used to be referred to in those days as "Rutilio's miracle."

A second thing that must have had an immediate impact on Archbishop Romero in those first days was the different reactions of various elements in the church. He was well aware that his appointment had not been well received by priests who practiced a more forward-moving pastoral ministry, by the base communities, or by anyone whose work was one of consciousness raising and liberation in the spirit of Medellin. He knew it had filled these persons with fear. He also knew of the jubilation that his appointment had inspired among comfortable Catholics—those who had been known to connive with the power groups that had attacked and calumniated his predecessor, Archbishop Chavez—and even among a little group of priests who had cozied up to those power groups. And so Archbishop Romero must have been very surprised when, in those first, difficult days, he saw that he was going to have to take real risks; the first group rallied to him and the second abandoned him. In the hour of truth, those whom he had regarded with suspicion, had attacked, and even had condemned were with him. The others, whom he had regarded as devout and orthodox, so prudent and "nonpolitical," apparently so faithful to whatever the church had to say, left him in the lurch, as Jesus' disciples had their master. They promptly began to criticize, attack, and disobey him, thereby showing their true colors: their apparent loyalty to the hierarchy did not go so far as to agree with their archbishop when he said things no longer to their liking, or when their particular interests were somehow threatened. . . .

A third factor in Archbishop Romero's conversion—the definitive factor, the one that kept him faithful to God's will to the end—was his people, a people of the poor. The poor very promptly showed him their acceptance, support, affection, and love. Surely he did not expect this when he was appointed archbishop. But the poor certainly hoped for an archbishop such as he proved to be. The fact is, as I have already remarked, that in El Salvador, as in so many other places in Latin America, before the church made an option for the poor, the poor had made an option for the church. They had found no one else to defend them, not in the government, not in the armed forces, not in the political parties, and not in private enterprise.

While Archbishop Romero was taking his first steps, making his first denunciations, making his first visits to the base communities, the poor fairly swarmed around him. He took them to his heart, and they were there to stay. And they took him to their own hearts, where he has remained to this day.

I do not propose to belabor this abundantly acknowledged, public point. I wish only to add that Archbishop Romero must have found in the poor what the prophet Isaiah contemplated in the Suffering Servant of Yahweh and St. Paul saw in the crucified Christ: light and salvation. The suffering of the poor must have shaken Archbishop Romero to his depths as he watched their oppression swell to such intolerable proportions. The poor were effectively calling for his conversion. But in offering him light and salvation, they also facilitated that conversion—and Archbishop Romero recognized this. For me there is no doubt that this is Archbishop Romero's last secret, and I shall reveal that secret. In one of his most felicitous expressions, in words of the kind that cannot be invented, but can only come from the heart, he said, "With this people, it is not difficult to be a good shepherd."

A New Experience of God

. . . I believe that Archbishop Romero, at the age of fifty-nine, not only underwent a conversion, but had a new experience of God. Never again would he be capable of separating God from the poor, or his faith in God from his defense of the poor. I believe he saw in God the prototype of his own option for the poor, and that that prototype demanded he put his option into practice. But I think his experience also enlightened him as to who God is. Why was he never shocked by new formulations of God's identity? He assimilated concepts like "God of life, God of the Reign, God of the poor," and so on, altogether naturally. He was particularly fond of the Gloria of the *Misa Salvadoreña,* which sings the praise of the God of life and condemns the gods of power and money.

Yet this costly, gladsome discovery of the God of the poor never induced Archbishop Romero to disparage in the least something I think must have been a constant in every aspect of his life: the mystery of God. From his new starting point in the poor, Archbishop Romero discovered that God is theirs—their defender, their liberator. Among the poor he discovered that God is God become small—a suffering God, a crucified God. But this also led him to sound the depths of the mystery of an ever-greater, transcendent God, the last reserve of truth, goodness, and humanity, on whom we human beings can rely. I do not know whether Archbishop Romero knew the words from Irenaeus . . ., *"Vita autem hominis, visio Dei."* . . . "And the life of the human being is the vision of God." But whether he knew the words or not, he communicated their content. Personally, I was profoundly struck—and I have tried to convey it in my writings—by his faith in God, his absolute conviction of God's reality, his utter conviction that the mystery of God is salvific for human beings, that it is good that there is a God, that we should be glad that there is a God. On February 10, 1980, in a situation that had become chaotic, in out-and-out confrontation with the government, the army, the oligarchy, and the United States,

Archbishop Romero was once more the courageous, implacable prophet, speaking of the things of this world and coming out in defense of an oppressed people. But in the same homily, and just as naturally as he had pronounced his historic denunciations, he spoke the following words: "Tell me, beloved brothers and sisters, that the fruit of today's sermon will be that each of us will encounter God, and that we shall live in the glory of his majesty and our littleness! . . . No human being has self-knowledge without having encountered God." . . .

The God of the poor and the mystery of God are what Archbishop Romero made present to all who were willing to listen. In El Salvador he restored respect for God. The poor listened to him, of course—what else is left to them, frequently, but their faith in God? But nonbelievers listened to him as well—those who at least respect God's name. And doubters listened to him, with gratitude that he was shedding light on something that had become darkness for them.   "Some Personal Reflections," 1–17

MAURA, ITA, DOROTHY, AND JEAN

I have stood by the bodies of Maura Clarke, Ita Ford, Dorothy Kazel, and Jean Donovan. Once more I felt what I have felt so often since the murder of Rutilio Grande, in 1977. Then, the martyrs had been a Jesuit priest—my friend and comrade—and two Aguilares campesinos. This time the martyrs were four American women missionaries: two Maryknoll sisters, an Ursuline sister, and a social worker from the diocese of Cleveland, Ohio. Between those two dates—March 12, 1977, and December 2, 1980—there has been martyrdom upon martyrdom—an endless procession of priests, seminarians, students, campesinos, teachers, workers, professionals, and intellectuals murdered for the faith in El Salvador.

Death has come to be the inseparable, dismal companion of our people. And yet, each time we gather to bid our martyrs farewell, the same feelings well up inside, surge to the surface again. First we are filled with indignation and grief, and we cry with the psalmist: "How long, O Lord? How long?" Then comes that feeling of determination and high resolve, and we pray with the psalmist: "Rejoice, Jerusalem. Your deliverance is at hand!"

This time, however, things are different. No one can conceal the new sensation we have. Not since the murder of Archbishop Romero (March 24, 1980) has there been a commotion like the one occasioned by *this* latest martyrdom. Neither within the country nor abroad has there been such a universal repudiation, such a feeling that God's patience must be exhausted and that this martyrdom is telling us that liberation is in the offing.

There were three hundred of us priests and sisters gathered in the chancery to hear Archbishop Rivera. His voice had a new and different ring, as he denounced the Security Forces of the Christian Democratic Junta. He tore the masks from their faces. He pointed the finger of shame and guilt. Once again, the truth was crystal clear. And with the truth came courage, and the Christian resolve to keep on, shoulder to shoulder with a massacred people, even if it meant that the church must march once more to the cross.

* * *

It was the first Christian Easter all over again. The horror, the abandonment, the solitude of Jesus' cross had driven the disciples to their refuge in the upper room. But Jesus' spirit was mightier than death, and it flung the doors wide apart. The disciples emerged stronger than before, determined to preach resurrection and life, determined to proclaim the good news of the reign of the poor. The archbishop's residence had been transformed into a latter-day upper room. The God of life was there. And that God was stronger than death, stronger than oppression and repression, stronger than ourselves and our fears and terrors. There, in the presence of four corpses, the Christian paradox came to life. Yes, where sin and crime had abounded, life and grace abounded even more.

This past Easter was a special celebration indeed. With this last murder the reservoirs of iniquity have over spilled their limits. The dams of evil have burst. We have seen everything in El Salvador. No barbarity would surprise us, we thought. But this time we were overwhelmed. Once more we witnessed the murder of the just, the innocent. But this time the murdered Christ was present in the person of four women, four missionaries, four Americans. This time the thick clouds of crime were pierced by a brand new light.

The murdered Christ is here in the person of four *women*. In the drama of the world, and the drama of the church, all the actors are human beings. We are all of us equal, as well as different, in God's eyes. And yet, the two together—equality and difference—are hard to come by in our history. Then suddenly, with these four dead bodies, we see something of it. Men and women are oppressed and repressed in El Salvador. Men and women have raised their lamentation to God and begged God to hear the cries wrung from them by their exploiters. Men and women have thrown in their lot with the struggle for liberation. And men and women have fallen in that struggle. Here is the most profound equality of all: equality in suffering and in hope.

By making themselves one with the archetypical Salvadoran woman, these four sisters made themselves one with the whole Salvadoran people. Woman is the procreator of humankind. But she is the creator of humanity—of humanness and humaneness—as well, in a specific manner all her own: in the delicacy of her service, her limitless self-donation, her affective and effective contact with the people, and that compassion of hers that simply will not rationalize the suffering of the poor. Woman is the creator of a courage that will never abandon the suffering, as these four sisters did not abandon their people when they saw the danger. . . . This fact points up the singular barbarity of their murder. It shows that barbarity for what it is. And it demonstrates the simplicity and gratuity of these women's self-sacrifice.

The murdered Christ is present here in the person of four *religious*. We hear a great deal about the renewal of the religious life today, in El Salvador as elsewhere. We hear a great deal about charisms and vows. And now these four dead bodies show us what a life of consecration to God today is all about. They make no fuss. They hold no grandiloquent harangues. They show us, simply, the basic element of all religious charism: service. Religious women today have been moving out more and more, reaching the most abandoned places, places where others cannot or will not go. They have drawn close to the poor, in genuineness and in truth, the poor of the slums, the poor of the working-class neighborhoods, and especially the poor campesinos. Consecration to God today means service and dedication to the poor.

Just as quietly, women religious have exercised their prophetic charism, which is part and parcel of the religious life. By their presence, by their activity, they have denounced the petrification of other echelons of the church. They have denounced the alienation of the hierarchy from Christian peoples. Above all, they have denounced the death-dealing sin that decimates the Salvadoran population. Therefore they have suffered the fate of the prophets, and shared the people's own lot: martyrdom. And so religious women, too, have their representatives among the martyrs of all social classes. They too have made an option for the poor, and therefore they too had to die.

The dead Christ is present among us in the person of four *Americans*. The United States is everywhere in El Salvador. We have U.S. businessmen and military experts. We have a U.S. embassy here to decide the fate of Salvadorans without consulting them. We have U.S. arms, we have U.S. helicopters to pursue and bombard the civilian population. But we have something else from the United States, too. We have American Christians, priests, and nuns. These have given us the best the United States has to offer: faith in Jesus instead of faith in the almighty dollar; love for persons instead of love for an imperialist plan; a thirst for justice instead of a lust for exploitation. With these four Americans, Christ, although he came from a far-off land, was no stranger in El Salvador. He was a Salvadoran, through and through.

In these four religious women, the churches of El Salvador and of the United States have become sister churches. After all, Christian action is helping others for their own sake, not blackmailing them with economic aid or babying them with paternalism. El Salvador gave these four sisters new eyes, and they beheld the crucified body of Christ in our people. El Salvador gave these four sisters new hands, and they healed Christ's wounds in the people of our land. The United States of America gave us four women who left their native land to give. And they gave all, in utter simplicity. They gave their very lives.

What has brought these two churches together? What has enabled the churches of El Salvador and the United States to contribute so much to the upbuilding of the world church? The poor. Service to the poor. How moved I was to hear from Peggy Healy, the Maryknoll sister who was a friend of the murdered sisters, that the high-ranking officials sent here by President Carter were to investigate not only the death of four American citizens, but the genocide of ten thousand Salvadorans. —"Maura, Ita, Dorothy, and Jean," 54–57

"I LOVED MY MARTYRED BROTHERS VERY MUCH"

I have often been asked to write something immediately after some tragedy happened in El Salvador: the murder of Rutilio Grande, of Archbishop Romero, of the four North American sisters, to name only the most prominent cases. All these were occasions for both sorrow and indignation. But in some way or another, we who survived managed to transform these feelings quite quickly into hope and service. In my case, this took the form, as we say, of analyzing the events theologically. This time it was different. In order to write you need a clear head and courage in your heart, but in this case, for days my head was just empty and my heart frozen.

Now, some time later, as I am gradually feeling calmer, I am setting out to write these reflections. I do it in grateful homage—a

small unnecessary homage perhaps—to my six martyred brothers. I am also doing it to try to bring some light and cheer to
those of us who are still in this world, a cruel world that murders
the poor and those who cast their lot with them, a world that
also tries to paralyze those who are alive by killing their hope.

I am writing personally, because at the moment, with my
memory of my murdered brothers still fresh in my mind, I cannot do it any other way. Later on will be the time to interpret
what happened in a more considered and analytical way, but
now I could not do it. And I prefer to do it this way because perhaps writing like this, under the impact of sorrow and my sense
of loss, I may be able to communicate a little of what hundreds
of thousands of Salvadorans have also felt. Between seventy
thousand and seventy-five thousand people have died in El Salvador, but now that it has hit home to me, I have felt something
of the sorrow and indignation that so many Salvadorans must
have felt, peasants, workers, students, and especially mothers,
wives, daughters, when their loved ones were killed.

First, I am going to relate simply what I felt when I heard
the news and during those first days, in a very personal way.
This experience is not important in itself, because it is only a
drop in the ocean of tears that is El Salvador, but perhaps it may
help to convey the pain of the Salvadoran people. After that I
shall offer some general reflections on my friends and various
important matters that their martyrdom raises. I shall speak of
them as a group, especially the five who worked in the Central
American University, the UCA, whom I knew best. I shall say a
bit more about Ignacio Ellacuría, because I lived with him for
longer and it was he who most often put into words what these
Jesuits accepted as fundamental in their lives and work.

"Something Terrible Has Happened"

From November 13 I was in Hua Hin, about two hundred
kilometers from Bangkok in Thailand, giving a short course on
christology. I was following on the radio the tragic events taking
place in El Salvador and I had managed to speak to the Jesuits

by telephone. They told me they were all well, and Ellacuría had just come back from Europe and entered the country with no problems. That same Monday 13 the army had searched our house, room by room, and the Archbishop Romero Center in the UCA, without further consequences.

Very late on the night of November 16—it would have been eleven o'clock in the morning in San Salvador—an Irish priest woke me up. While half asleep, he had heard news on the BBC saying that something serious had happened to the UCA Jesuits in El Salvador. To reassure himself, he had phoned London and then he woke me up. "Something terrible has happened," he told me. "It is not very clear, but it seems they have murdered a Jesuit from the UCA; I don't know whether it is the Rector. London will give you more information."

On the way to the telephone, I thought, although I did not want to believe it, that they had murdered Ignacio Ellacuría. Ellacuría, a brave and stubborn man, was not a demagogue but a genuine prophet in his writings, and ever more publicly on television. A little while ago an ordinary Salvadoran woman had said to me after seeing him on television: "Not since they murdered Archbishop Romero has anyone spoken out so plainly in this country." All these thoughts were going through my head on my short walk to the phone.

At the other end of the telephone, in London, was a great friend of mine and of all the Jesuits in El Salvador, a man who has shown great solidarity with our country and our church. He began with these words: "Something terrible has happened." "I know," I replied, "Ellacuría." But I did not know. He asked me if I was sitting down and had something to write with. I said I had and then he told me what had happened. "They have murdered Ignacio Ellacuría." I remained silent and did not write anything, because I had already been afraid of this. But my friend went on: "They have murdered Segundo Montes, Ignacio Martin-Baro, Amando López, Juan Ramón Moreno, and Joaquin Lopez y Lopez." My friend read the names slowly and each of them reverberated like a hammer blow that I received in total helplessness.

I was writing them down, hoping that the list would end after each name. But after each name came another, on to the end. The whole community, my whole community, had been murdered. In addition, two women had been murdered with them. They were living in a little house at the entrance to the university and because they were afraid of the situation they asked the fathers if they could spend the night in our house because they felt safer there. They were also mercilessly killed. Their names are Julia Elba, who had been the Jesuits' cook for years, and her fifteen-year-old daughter Celina. As in the case of Rutilio Grande, when two peasants were murdered with him, this time two ordinary Salvadoran women died with the Jesuits.

Then my friend in London started giving me the details that were coming through in international telegrams. The killers were about thirty men dressed in military uniform. He told me they had taken three of the Jesuits out into the garden and tortured and machine-gunned them there. The other three and the two women they had machine-gunned in their beds. My friend could hardly go on speaking. Like many others during those days, he had no words to express what had happened. He managed to give me a few words of comfort and solidarity, and finally he wondered what strange providence had seen to it that I was not in our house at the time.

I spent several hours, or rather several days, unable to react. As I said at the beginning, on other tragic occasions we recovered our courage fairly quickly and were fired with a sense of service, which made us active, in some way alleviating our sorrow by pushing the scenes of terror out of our heads. The Masses we celebrated for the martyrs even filled us with joy. But this time, for me, it was different. The distance made me feel helpless and alone. And the six murdered Jesuits were my community, they were really my family. We had lived, worked, suffered, and enjoyed ourselves together for many years. Now they were dead.

I do not think I have ever felt anything like it. I told the Irish priest who was with me that night that it was the most important thing that had happened to me in my whole life. I do not think that is an exaggeration. My long years in El Salvador, my work, including risks and conflicts, the difficult situations I had been through, even my religious life as a priest, seemed much less important things than the death of my brothers. They did not seem very real in comparison with these deaths. I felt a real breakdown in my life and an emptiness that nothing could fill. During those moments I remembered the biblical passage about the mothers of the murdered children who wept and could not be comforted. When I thought about things in my normal life, writing, talks, and classes, the things I had been doing for the last sixteen years in El Salvador and might be doing in the future, it all seemed unreal to me, with nothing to do with the reality. The most real reality—as I have often written from El Salvador—is the life and death of the poor. From thousands of miles away, and although I was still alive, the death of my brothers was a reality, compared to which everything else seemed little or nothing. Or rather, a reality that forced me to look at everything else from its standpoint. The church, the Society of Jesus, were not for me in those moments realities in terms of which—as it were, from a distance—I could understand or interpret their deaths, but the reverse. As a result of these deaths all those realities became questions for me and, very slowly—and I say this with gratitude—answers too to what is most fundamental in our lives: God, Jesus, vocation, the people of El Salvador.

I kept asking myself too why I was alive, and the Irish priest who was with me asked me the same question. I wanted to answer with the traditional words: "I am not worthy." But really there was no answer to that "why?" and I did not dwell on the question. Instead I began to have a feeling of irreparable loss. The UCA will never be the same, and I shall never be the same. After living and working with these brothers for so many years, it had become second nature to me to rely on them for my own life and work. Whatever idea, whatever plan, came into my head, always ended the same way: but they are not there anymore. Ellacuría is not there anymore, to finish the book we were editing together. Juan Ramón [Moreno] is no longer there to finish the next issue of the *Revista latinoamericana de teología*. Nacho [Martín-Baro] is no longer there to give the psychology of religion course I had asked him to give for the master's in theology. [Segundo] Montes is no longer there to understand the problems of the refugees and human rights. Lolo—that's what we called Fr. Joaquin Lopez y Lopez—is no longer there: he was usually silent, but had a great feel for the thoughts and hopes of the poor persons he worked with in the *Fe y Alegria* education program. The examples I have given are not important in themselves, of course, but I give them to show that I had lost the direct links that connected me to real life. And I remembered from my years studying philosophy that a writer (I do not remember who) defined—I am not sure if it was death or hell—as the total absence of relationships.

This was my experience in the first hours and days. It was my strongest sensation, beyond any doubt, but it was not the only one. The next morning the people in the course came up to me and embraced me in silence, many of them in tears. One of them told me that the death of my brothers was the best explanation and confirmation of the class we had held the previous day about Jesus, Yahweh's suffering servant, and the crucified people. The comment cheered me a little, not because it referred approvingly to my theology, of course, but because it linked my Jesuit brothers with Jesus and the oppressed. That same morning we had a Mass in Hua Hin with an altar decked with flowers in the beautiful Asian style, with the name of El Salvador written on it and eight candles, which people from different Asian and African countries—who were acquainted with sorrow and death—lit in turn while I spoke the names of the eight victims. That night in another city five hours away by car, I had another Mass with various Jesuits and many lay coworkers working with refugees from Vietnam, Burma, Cambodia, the Philippines, Korea. . . . They also knew about suffering and could understand what had happened in El Salvador. On Saturday and Sunday back in Bangkok, I gave two talks—as I had been asked to give beforehand—on Jesus and the poor. Personally I did not feel much like speaking, but I thought I owed it to my brothers and talking about them was the best possible way of presenting the life and death of Jesus of Nazareth and his commitment to the poor today. Of course in Thailand, a country with a tiny number of Christians, someone asked me ingenuously and incredulously: "Are there really Catholics who murder priests in El Salvador?"

So it was not all darkness and being alone. I began to hear the reactions in many places, the solidarity of many Jesuits all over the world, the clear words of Archbishop Rivera, the promise by Fr. Kolvenbach, our Father General, to come to El Salvador for Christmas, the immediate offer by various Jesuits from other countries to come to El Salvador and continue the work of those who had been murdered, the Mass in the Gesu, the Jesuit church in Rome, with about six hundred priests at the altar, another Mass in Munich with more than six thousand students, Masses in the USA, Spain, England, Ireland, and many more all over the world. I also received cards and telephone calls, full of tears and sorrow, but also full of love and gratitude to the six Jesuits. When they told me about the funeral Mass in the Archbishop Romero chapel, with Jesuits determined to carry on the work of the UCA, little by little I came out of the dark and got my courage back. From what I can tell, the human and Christian reaction to this murder has been unique, only comparable perhaps to the reaction to Archbishop Romero's murder. Politically there is no doubt that this murder has had the most repercussions since Archbishop Romero's. In several countries, they tell me, nothing has so galvanized the Jesuits as these martyrs. If this has been so, we can say without triumphalism that this martyrdom has already begun to produce good, and this is what keeps up our hope now, even though our sorrow and sense of loss has not diminished.

I have described this experience because I want to say that now I understand a little better what this world's victims mean. The figures—seventy thousand in El Salvador—are horrifying, but when these victims have particular names and are persons who have been very close to you, the sorrow is terrible. I have told this story because I also wanted to say simply that I loved my murdered and martyred brothers very much. I am very grateful to them for what they gave me in their lives and for what they have given me in their death. Finally I have told the story so that what I am going on to say can be more easily understood. I am not going to say anything extraordinary, but things that are well known. I do so honestly and sincerely, not as a matter of course but with the conviction aroused by this tragic event.

—*"Companions of Jesus,"* 3–9

THE CRUCIFIED PEOPLE MAKE CHRIST PRESENT IN HISTORY

The Crucified People as Yahweh's Suffering Servant

The christological interpretation of the crucified people developed in Latin America from the analysis of similarity between the crucified people and the figure of Yahweh's Suffering Servant. Two Salvadoran martyrs did this and they knew what they were talking about. Archbishop Romero said that Jesus Christ, the liberator, "is so closely identified with the people that interpreters of scripture cannot tell whether Yahweh's Servant proclaimed by Isaiah is the suffering people or Christ who comes to redeem us." Ignacio Ellacuría said: "This crucified people is the historical continuation of Yahweh's Servant, whom the sin of the world continues to deprive of his human face. The powerful of this world continue to strip them of everything, to snatch everything from them, even their lives, especially their lives." This theological interpretation of the crucified people as Yahweh's Suffering Servant has taken root in Latin America, while in other places it may still seem too bold or simply to be unscholarly pious talk. This interpretation has taken root through insight rather than through exegetical analysis, but it is possible to show that the insight is sure and not arbitrary. . . .

* * *

(c) The crucified people as the presence of Christ crucified in history. I have analyzed the crucified people's situation in relation to the Suffering Servant through its historical similarity to what the Servant Songs say. But the crucified people, also, make Christ present in history through the fact that they are a people and not just an individual. They make Christ present first and foremost through the bare fact of being massively on the cross. But they also make him present because, like the lamb of God, they carry the sin of the world and by carrying it they offer light and salvation to all. This insight does not come from pure biblical textual analysis, but nevertheless I think it is true.

Of course, my presentation of the crucified people here may be open to question. But we must be aware of the fundamental issue, which is much more important: it would be idle to say that Christ crucified has a body in history and not identify it in some way.

From the viewpoint of christology we must ask what this body is. I believe the christology of the cross described above helps us to find it in the crucified people and to see the saving mystery of the cross in them. Therefore we can say that the crucified people are Christ's crucified body in history. But the opposite is also true: the present day crucified people allow us to know the crucified Christ better. He is the head of the body and in him we can see Yahweh's Suffering Servant and understand his mystery of light and salvation.

* * *

Martyrdom by Analogy: The "Martyred People"

Understanding martyrdom in terms of Jesus' death clarifies what is fundamental about it. This also means we must speak of martyrdom by analogy. The analogy is necessary, because today many people are dying in a context similar to that of Jesus, whereas others are dying in different contexts. To illustrate the analogy, let us describe three typical situations, although they cannot always be adequately distinguished.

(i) At present there are many martyrs who structurally reproduce the martyrdom *of* Jesus. Examples are the martyrdom of
Archbishop Romero and many other priests, nuns, catechists,
delegates of the word, students, trade unionists, peasants, workers, teachers, journalists, doctors, lawyers. . . . Subjectively, some
may have been holier than others, of course, but in their lives
they defended the Kingdom and attacked the anti-Kingdom,
they exercised prophetic violence and were put to death. So they
are like Jesus; and in them we see clearly what I have called the
Christian notion of martyrdom. Nevertheless, there are other
kinds of death that are not exactly the same as the above. In
them the "vulnerability" or "freedom," which are characteris-
tics of true martyrdom according to the official definition, and
appear in the death of Jesus, are not as obviously present. So we
have to ask whether they can also be called martyrs by analogy.

(ii) There are many Christians in the popular organizations,
who defend the Kingdom by open struggle and make use of some
sort of violence—beyond the prophetic word—social, political
and even armed violence. Many of them are put to death, but
not all of them are defenseless. In order to tell whether they
can be called martyrs, we have to take into account—supposing
the ethical legitimacy of the various kinds of struggle—the central criterion for martyrdom: that it should be unjustly inflicted
death for love's sake. From this viewpoint Aquinas saw no difficulty in considering a soldier's death as a possible martyrdom,
since "the good of the republic is the highest of goods" and
"any human good can be a cause of martyrdom insofar as it is
referred to God."

Whether these deaths are martyrdom or not may be considered a *quaestio disputata,* and in the end only God can judge
where great love has been shown. But it is worth reflecting on
the question because we cannot ignore the countless Christians
who struggle politically, socially and even by taking up arms for
love of the people, and who are ready to lay down their lives
generously for love. Only God knows how great their love is
and whether and how they overcome the dehumanizing dangers,
the mystique of violence condemned by Archbishop Romero,

and the negative by-products generated by struggle, especially armed struggle. However, they can reproduce a central element of martyrdom: laying down one's life for love, and so they can share in martyrdom by analogy. In any case, it is very important that in death their dignity is maintained, whether they are called "fallen" or "martyrs" and that their mothers at least have this comfort.

(iii) Finally, there are the masses who are innocently and anonymously murdered, even though they have not used any explicit form of violence, even verbal. They do not actively lay down their lives to defend the faith, or even, directly, to defend God's Kingdom. They are the peasants, children, women and old people, above all, who die slowly day after day and die violently with incredible cruelty and totally unprotected, as we saw in the meditation on the crucified people. They are simply killed and massacred. And they die without freedom, if not through necessity.

I have called these crucified people Yahweh's Servant, but there is no word in church language to express what, if any, excellence there is in their death, and they are not called martyrs because they lack the requisite of having given their lives "freely." This is because the poor do not have freedom (just as they often do not have the material conditions to possess the kind of virtues required for canonization). We must find some solution to this paradox so that we do not fall into the absurd position of saying that the faith has nothing to say to these passively crucified people and they have nothing important to say to the faith. In order to be able to call them martyrs we must understand martyrdom analogically, and we also must give deep thought to what is martyrdom's *analogatum princeps* [primary analogue] and think about it looking at the cross of Jesus.

In comparison with Jesus' death, the deaths of these murdered masses, descriptively and historically speaking, do not so much illustrate the active character of the struggle against the anti-Kingdom or the freedom with which this is undertaken. But they do illustrate their historical innocence—because they have done nothing to deserve death except to be poor—and vulnerable—because they are not even physically capable of avoiding it. Above all, their deaths make clear that it is these masses who are unjustly burdened with a sin which has been annihilating them little by little throughout their lives and annihilates them finally in their death. Whether they are called martyrs or not, these masses who are oppressed during their lives and die in massacres are the ones who illustrate best the vast suffering of the world.

If we consider martyrdom in terms of the anti-Kingdom's response to those who struggle actively for the Kingdom, the *analogatum princeps* of the martyr is that exemplified by Archbishop Romero. If we consider it in terms of really bearing the sin of the anti-Kingdom, the *analogatum princeps* becomes the unprotected masses, who are put to death in huge numbers innocently and anonymously. Earlier we called them Yahweh's Suffering Servant, now we call them the "martyred people." They are the ones who most abundantly and cruelly "fill up in their flesh what is lacking in Christ's passion." They are the Suffering Servant and they are the crucified Christ today.

—*Jesus the Liberator*, 255, 264, 269–71

THE CRUCIFIED PEOPLES: YAHWEH'S SUFFERING SERVANT TODAY

In Memory of Ignacio Ellacuría

Ignacio Ellacuría admired Jürgen Moltmann's well-known book, *The Crucified God*, but he made a point of stressing another much more urgent theological idea: the crucified people. . . . It is necessary to speak of these crucified peoples in relation to 1992. . . . [But] the sole object of all this talk must be to bring them down from the *cross*.

The Crucified Peoples: A Horrifying Fact

When what is obvious in others—the crucified peoples—shows us what we are, we tend to ignore it, cover it up, or distort it, because it simply terrifies us. . . . So let us start by discovering the covered-up reality of our world. . . . At the origin of what we call Latin America today there lies an original and originating sin. To give one single fact: Some seventy years after 1492, the indigenous population had been reduced to 15 percent; many of their cultures had been destroyed and subjected to anthropological death. This was a colossal disaster. . . .

So there was a historical disaster, and we have to give it a name. Our current language calls these peoples "Third World," "the South," "developing countries." These designations are attempting to say that something is wrong, but such language does not communicate how wrong. Therefore we need to speak of crucified peoples. . . .

Crucified peoples is useful and necessary language at the real level of fact, because *cross* means death, and death is what the Latin American peoples are subjected to in thousands of ways. . . . It is useful and necessary language at the historical-ethical level because *cross* expresses a type of death actively inflicted. To die crucified does not mean simply to die, but to be put to death; it means that there are victims and there are executioners. It means that there is a very grave sin. . . . However much people try to soften the fact, the truth is that the Latin American peoples' cross has been inflicted on them by the various empires that have taken power over the continent: the Spanish and Portuguese yesterday, the U.S. and its allies today; whether by armies or economic systems, or the imposition of cultures and religious views, in connivance with the local powers.

It is useful and necessary language at the religious level because *cross*—Jesus suffered death on the cross and not any other death—evokes sin and grace, condemnation and salvation, human action and God's action. From a Christian point of view, God himself makes himself present in these crosses, and the crucified peoples become the principal sign of the times. "This sign [of God's presence in our world] is always the historically crucified people."[1] Crucified peoples exist. It is necessary and urgent to see our world this way. And it is right to call them this,

---

1. Casaldáliga, "The 'Crucified' Indians—A Case of Anonymous Collective Martyrdom," 51.

because this language stresses their historical tragedy and their meaning for faith.

The Crucified People as Yahweh's Suffering Servant

In Latin America . . . the crucified people are the actualization of Christ crucified, the true servant of Yahweh. The crucified people and Christ, Yahweh's servant, refer to and explain each other. The theology of the crucified people as Yahweh's suffering servant includes not only the servant as victim . . . but also the servant's saving role in history: . . . To grasp this theology, we need only read the songs of Yahweh's servant . . . in the form of a meditation.[2]

What do the songs say about the servant? Above all, he is a "man of sorrows acquainted . . . with grief," and this is the normal condition of the crucified people: hunger, sickness, slums, frustration through lack of education, health, employment . . . And if their penalties are innumerable in normal times, "peace time," as it is called, they increase even more when, like the servant, they decide to "establish justice and right." Then repression falls on them and the verdict, "guilty of death." . . .

It is said of the servant that "he was oppressed and he was afflicted yet he opened not his mouth," that he died in total meekness. . . . Who knows the seventy thousand assassinated in El Salvador and the eighty thousand in Guatemala? What word is uttered by the children of Ethiopia and the three hundred million in India living in dire poverty? There are thousands and millions who do not say a word. It is not known how they live or how they died. Their names are not known—Julia Elba and Celina are known because they were murdered with the Jesuits. Even their number is not known. . . .

The crucified people are this suffering servant of Yahweh today. This fact is covered up, because like the servant, the people are innocent. "He had done no violence and there was no deceit in his mouth." The servant not only proclaims the truth

---

2. Sobrino, "Meditación ante el pueblo crucificado," 93–104.

of the crucified people, but also the truth about their killers. All of us can and must look at ourselves reflected in the crucified people in order to grasp our deepest reality. As in a mirror, we can see what we are by what we produce.

And we have to be very aware of this in 1992. Some will recall the advances in science and democracy that the Western world has brought, and the church will remember the preaching of the gospel. . . . But at the hour of truth, unless we profoundly accept the truth of the crucified peoples and the fundamental responsibility of successive empires for their crucifixion, we will miss the main fact. That is, that in this world there is still enormous sin. Sin is what killed the servant—and sin is what continues to kill God's children. . . . In a typically Spanish turn of phrase, Ellacuría summed up what successive empires have done to the Latin American continent: "they have left it like a Christ"—they have made a Christ of it.[3]

The Salvation the Crucified Peoples Bring

The foregoing theology is fundamental . . . as an expression of the current problem of theodicy, "how to do theology after Auschwitz." However, in Latin America, we add a second perspective belonging more specifically to liberation theology: We must bring the, crucified peoples down from the cross. . . . This is the marrow of liberation theology. . . . The crucified people themselves are bearers of salvation. The one chosen by God to bring salvation is the servant, which increases the scandal. . . .

Liberation theology has tried to analyze what salvation and what historical salvation is brought by the servant, and Ellacuría did so with great rigor and vigor in his work *The Crucified People*, which he subtitled "an essay in historical soteriology." Understanding what salvation is brought by the crucified people's suffering is not only or principally a matter of speculation and interpretation of texts. It is a matter of grasping the reality.

---

3. Ellacuría, *Quinto Centenario* (n. 1), 58.

The Light the Crucified Peoples Bring

God says of the servant that he will set him up as a "light for the nations" (Isa. 42:6; 49:6). Today this light is to show the nations what they really are. . . . Ellacuría expressed this graphically in various ways. He said bluntly, using a medical metaphor, that in order to test the health of the First World it was necessary to do a "copro-analysis," that is, to examine its feces, because it is the reality of the crucified peoples that appears in that analysis, and their reality reveals that of those who produce them. He also said that the Third World, offers a great advantage over the First World in throwing light on where we ought to be going.

> From my viewpoint—and this can be one that is both prophetic and paradoxical at once—the US is much worse off than Latin America. Because the US has a solution but in my opinion it is a bad solution, both for them and for the world as a whole. On the other hand, in Latin America there are no solutions, there are only problems. But however painful it is, it is better to have problems than to have a wrong solution for the future of history.[4]

The solution offered by the First World today is factually wrong, because it is unreal; it is not universalizable. And it is ethically wrong, because it is dehumanizing for all, for them and for the Third World.

Finally he said that the Third World offered light on what historical utopia must be today . . . a "civilization of poverty,"[5] all sharing austerely in the earth's resources so that they can stretch to everybody. This achieves what the First World does not offer: fellowship and with it, meaning of life. . . .

---

4. Ibid.
5. Ignacio Ellacuría, "The Kingdom of God and Unemployment in the Third World," *Concilium* 160 (1982): 91–96.

The Salvation the Crucified Peoples Bring

The crucified peoples also offer positive salvation. Obviously, this is scandalous, but unless we accept it in principle, it will be pointless to repeat that there is salvation in the servant, that the crucified Christ has taken upon himself and got rid of the sin of the world.

Above all, the crucified peoples offer values that are not offered elsewhere. . . . Puebla said it with chilling clarity, although Western countries and churches have taken very little notice: The poor have evangelizing potential. This potential is spelled out, as "the gospel values of solidarity, service, simplicity and readiness to receive God's gift" (no. 1147). In historical language, the poor have a humanizing potential because they offer community against individualism, co-operation against selfishness, simplicity against opulence, and openness to transcendence against blatant positivism, so prevalent in the civilization of the Western world. It is true, of course, that not all the poor offer this, but it is also true that they do offer it and, structurally speaking, in a form not offered by the First World.

The crucified peoples also offer hope, foolish or absurd, it might be said; because it is the only thing they have left, others argue. But once again, it is there, and it must not be trivialized by other worlds. . . . The very fact that hope arises and rearises in history shows that history has a current of hope running through it which is available to all. The bearers of this current of hope are the crucified peoples.

The crucified peoples offer great love. . . . Latin America's innumerable martyrs show that love is possible because it is real, and great love is possible because many have shown it. . . . The crucified peoples are ready to forgive their oppressors. They do not want to triumph over them but share with them. To those who come to help them, they open their arms and accept them and thus, even without knowing it themselves, they forgive them. . . .

The crucified peoples have generated solidarity—human beings and Christians mutually supporting one another, in this way and that, open to one another, giving and receiving one another's best. . . . On a small scale, it offers a model of how people and churches can relate to one another in a human and Christian way.

Finally, the crucified peoples offer faith, a way of being the church and a more genuine, Christian, and relevant holiness for the world today, that gives more of Jesus. . . . It is paradoxical, but it is true. The crucified peoples offer light and salvation. Both can be had in 1992 by those who declare themselves their discoverers, although they have mostly been their coverersup. Not to receive them would be ungrateful and idiotic; it would be the most radical way of ruining the 1992 "celebrations. . . .

I wish to end with the words with which Ignacio Ellacuría concluded his reflections in 1992. He was not in the least inclined to ahistorical idealism or purely transcendental statements that could not be located in history.

> I wish to state the following. Far from causing discouragement and despair, all this martyr's blood spilt in El Salvador and the whole of Latin America infuses our people with a new spirit of struggle and new hope. In this sense, if we are not a "new world" or a "new continent," we are clearly and demonstrably a continent of hope, which is a highly interesting symptom of a future new relation to other continents which do not have hope—the only thing they have is fear.[6]

> —"The Crucified Peoples: Yahweh's Suffering Servant Today," 49–57;
> translated by Dinah Livingstone

"I HAVE SEEN GOD"

You ask me if some image of God remains engraved in my mind. Indeed, the answer is "yes." In the mid-1980s I used to visit the

---

6. Ellacuría, *Quinto Centenario* (n. 1), 16.

San Roque shelter on the outskirts of San Salvador. There was the basement of a church where men, women and children lived literally crammed tight. They were so terrified of the security forces that they kept the doors closed all the time. In spite of this, however, bullet holes were visible on the walls from shots fired from outside. The basement had no windows or access to the outside, so that the refugees could see neither the light of the sun nor the moon. I remember that there were 11-month-old babies who had never in their lives seen natural light. Once, while celebrating a Holy Week liturgy in this environment, there was a woman whose face remains engraved in my memory. She was middle-aged, without being able to be more precise. Her gaze was a blend of accumulated suffering, serenity, beauty, dignity and hope. That is the image. And without knowing why, I said to myself these words: "I have seen God."   —"A Su Aire," 499–500

3

Following Jesus as the Way to Christ

Sobrino says in the introduction to his two-volume Christology, "I have done nothing more than—starting from Jesus—to elevate the reality we are living to the level of a theological concept; to theorize about a Christological faith that we see as real faith; to present Christ, the great witness to God, starting of course from the theological sources, . . . but also from the cloud of witnesses who illumine that testimony par excellence. For this reason, in spite of everything, this book is written with hope and joy."[1] Thus, Sobrino's reflections on Jesus Christ should be seen as opening a window on the joy and hope of the encounter with the Mystery of God in the suffering people of El Salvador by those who love them.

After initial reflections on the nature of Sobrino's Christological project, the chapter proceeds to the startling claim that "Christ has appeared again in Latin America." It then moves to Sobrino's assertion that the "Church of the poor," which emerges from God's "preferential option for the poor" discerned at Medellín in 1968, should be seen as a "wellspring of knowledge about Jesus Christ." This, in turn, creates the need for "a new christology," capable of correlating the encounter with God in the historical reality of the poor with that of Jesus Christ. Here we follow Sobrino as he builds on Ellacuría's fundamental

---

1. Jon Sobrino, *Jesucristo liberador: Lectura histórica-teológica de Jesús de Nazaret*, 30, my translation. See Sobrino, *Jesus the Liberator*, 8.

theology to assert that a truly Latin American Christology must (1) take "into account the historical reality of Jesus,"[2] (2) build on the insight that "the historical life of Jesus is the fullest revelation of the Christian God," and (3) explain how the defining aspects of the historical reality of Jesus constitute a salvation in history for Latin America. We also discover Rahner's influence on Sobrino's understanding of the crucified people, a concept that he believes was jointly discovered by Ignacio Ellacuría and Archbishop Romero. Building on Ellacuría's interpretation of Rahner's theology of symbol, Sobrino asserts (1) that the historical reality of Jesus is the real sign of the Word made flesh and (2) that the crucified peoples of today are the historical continuation of God's self-offer in the life, death, and resurrection of Jesus. As a result, Sobrino argues that the historical Jesus is the way to Christ, both in the New Testament and today.

In the end, however, Sobrino insists that it is the historical reality of the sometimes painful, sometimes joyful, encounter with God in the crucified people (which we heard about in Chapter 2), that shapes his reflection on the saving Mystery of Jesus Christ. Summarizing his approach in a letter to a young Jesuit, Sobrino writes,

> My Christology fundamentally says that Jesus Christ is a good news, a euaggelion. This is the impression that I have, and I think it is important to make note of it because that is, in my opinion, what is most original in a Christology of mercy, the cross, and martyrdom. In other words, cross and martyrdom refer not only to "sin," but also to "grace." This seems to me the most important contribution from the "Salvadoran school" of theology (Ignacio Ellacuría, Monseñor Romero . . .).[3]

Sobrino then explains that our encounter with the risen Jesus in the crucified people of today places a demand that changes us,

---

2. Ignacio Ellacuría, *Freedom Made Flesh: The Mission of Christ and His Church*, 27.

3. Jon Sobrino, "Letter to Hartono Budi," 2.

referring us back to the historical reality of Jesus and pushing us forward to live as Jesus lived (taking the crucified people down from the cross).

The chapter ends with a personal letter in which Sobrino explains, "Though the martyrdom of the Jesuits obviously caused a special psychological impact, it has not been the only decisive moment." Sobrino's idea is that when we take the crucified people down from the cross, we are drawn into the work of the Trinity in the world and the Mystery of God, making us more like Jesus who embodies what it means to live as though we believe in the resurrection. Sobrino asserts, "Perhaps in this aspect, the most important martyrdom for my theology was that of Archbishop Romero," which helped him "to conceive of martyrdom as a recapitulation of the life, praxis, and cross of Jesus, and also to conceive of it as good news, due to the affinity it has with the crucified people."

WHY A NEW "CHRISTOLOGY?"

Sobrino: I wrote *Jesus Christ Liberator* [*Jesus the Liberator*] as part of a project of Latin American theologians dealing with fundamental themes [in Catholic theology]. But really, this "christology" is not new, and I do not say this just because the title is old.[4] Unfortunately, the world continues to be a situation of oppression. There are more poor people in the world today than yesterday. I have written this book so that, at least, this oppression cannot continue in the name of Jesus.

Where is the originality of this christology?

Sobrino: I think that the treatment of idols, realities that are not only ignored, but covered up in Europe, is interesting. What needs to be said about Jesus is not only that he gives himself and is faithful to the Father, but that he combats the idols, a topic that is completely current.

What is truly original is the last chapter. Christologists clearly speak about the cross, and a few speak about the crucified God, but they do not usually speak about the crucified people. They

---

4. Leonardo Boff, *Jesucristo el liberador*.

do not speak about the continuation of martyrdom in the body of Christ, which is the Church. This is how I conclude the first volume of the christology.

This christology has emerged from many hours of study, but also from personal and pastoral experiences. What have been the lived experiences that influenced you in writing this book?

Sobrino: I live in a country where there are two fundamental realities. First: they have killed 75,000 people in recent years, including people close to me like Archbishop Romero and the UCA Jesuits. That makes one think. Suffering makes you think. Second: it is very surprising that commitment, hope, and dedication would spout up among the people in the midst of this cross. There is life in the midst of this death. This also stimulates thought.

Karl Rahner used to say that we human beings are a deficient way of being Christ. The "deficient" aspect is easily understood, but the "ways of being Christ" is what I have seen in these people.

To whom is this christology addressed?

Sobrino: In truth, the audience is people with a certain culture. The book is not for a typical peasant who lives in El Salvador. But it certainly wants to be a stimulus for those who fight for the Kingdom of God and see death nearby.

For the European or First World reader, it might serve as a jolt to help them get out of agnosticism. I refer to that suspension of judgment about everything as if nothing was really important.

The book is an invitation to follow Jesus, and that invitation is Good News which gives meaning to life. My ultimate hope is that it helps the poor of this world.

What features of Jesus should be highlighted in order to evangelize this world?

Sobrino: The priority for me is to be honest about reality, or, in more traditional terms, to ground oneself in reality. The biggest problem is that, in talking about other things, we should not overlook what is primary: the reality of this world. Utopia can be discussed, but the reality is that there are almost three billion people who live with terrible hunger. Jesus of Nazareth is honest about reality. This is what most attracts my attention about Jesus.

The prevailing dishonesty is not due to ill will, or because, for example, politicians or bishops are bad, but rather because everything is set up to hide the underlying reality.

This book ends with the cross. What hope does the crucified one bring to our world?

Sobrino: The cross, similar to the one Jesus, which is so present today in many places, is hope because it opens a horizon. The tragedy of this world is that great loves are put to an end by death. And that is because this world is one of enormous structural selfishness. The fact that there might be a great love similar to that of Jesus, carried all the way to the end, that is Good News, and that creates hope.

—"Hablando con Jon Sobrino, Hacer Creible la Fe," 16;
translated by Robert Lassalle-Klein

"CHRIST HAS APPEARED AGAIN IN LATIN AMERICA"

In recent years Christ has appeared again in Latin America. He has granted many Christians the grace of "seeing" him in the poor, and these visionaries have become, along with the visionaries of the New Testament, "witnesses" who are ready for a new mission that will shape a new Church or a new form of existence as Church. It is this new reality that I want to describe. . . .

The Spirit of Jesus is in the poor and, with them as his point of departure, he re-creates the entire Church. If this truth is understood in all its depth and in an authentically trinitarian perspective, it means that the history of God advances indefectibly by way of the poor; that the Spirit of Jesus takes historical flesh in the poor; and that the poor show the direction of history that is in accord with God's plan. "The union of God with human beings as we see this in Jesus Christ is historically a union with human beings of a God who basically pours himself out into the world of the poor."

For this profound reason I maintain that the Church of the poor is not a Church for the poor but a Church that must be formed on the basis of the poor and that must find in them the principle of its structure, organization, and mission. For the same reason I maintain that this Church does not conceive of the poor as "part" of itself, even a privileged part, but thinks of them rather as the "center" of the whole.

This means that the poor are the authentic *theological source* for understanding Christian truth and practice and therefore the constitution of the Church. The poor are those who confront the Church both with its basic theological problem and with the direction in which the solution to the problem is to be found. For the poor pose the problem of *seeking* God without presupposing that the Church possesses him once and for all. At the same time they offer the Church the place for *finding* him. Christian truth becomes a concrete universal when seen in terms of the poor. In the poor it acquires the potential that theology will develop for an understanding of history as a whole. In the poor we find the primordial conformity with the truth in its evangelical sources. With the poor as its starting point Christian practice recovers its concreteness, direction, and meaning; the poor have the final say about what is ultimate in Christianity—namely, love—about what love really is, about its necessary historical mediations, about its different expressions. The Christian understanding of sin becomes concrete when seen from the vantage point of the poor, for they suffer it, as no one else does, in their own flesh. They make it clear that sin brings death, and they show what kind of death it brings and what kind of hierarchy reigns in death.

When the poor are at the center of the Church, they give direction and meaning to everything that legitimately (by the standard of Christian tradition) and necessarily (by the standard of the structure of any association of human beings) constitutes the concrete Church: its preaching and activity, its administration, its cultural, dogmatic, theological, and other structures. The poor in no sense cause a "reduction" of ecclesial reality but rather are a source of "concretization" for everything ecclesial.

The establishment of the Church of the poor presupposes a willingness to focus specifically on those who at a given historical moment make up the poor and to overcome the frequent temptation to deal with them in such general terms that in fact they vanish from view.

For my purposes here it is enough to keep in mind that "the identity of these poor in the real situation of the Third World is not a problem whose solution requires scriptural exegesis or sociological analysis of historical theory. . . . No self-serving equivocations are admissible in face of the self-evident fact: the real situation of the majority of the human race." One indisputable merit of the Puebla Conference (México) was to have displayed in a concrete way the faces of these poor: peasants, workers, slum dwellers, the persecuted, the tortured. Today, as in the days of Isaiah and Jesus, these poor are those to whom the Good News is primarily addressed. By their material and historical situation they are in the best position to understand what the Good News is about. And it is these same poor, I say, who are the inspirational and organizational center of the Church. I shall not here expatiate on the fact that by reason of their material condition they are apt subjects for "spiritual poverty" and therefore able to realize the human ideal set down in the Scriptures. The important thing to remember is that a Church that arises in solidarity with the poor protests against their material poverty as being an expression of the world's sin, engages in a struggle against this poverty as a form of liberation, and allows itself to be affected by this poverty and its consequences as an expression of its own kenosis. Such a Church is indeed a Church of the poor.

There is no question here of idealizing, much less sacralizing, the poor. The point is rather to recover an ancient idea that has been often repeated in Catholic theology: certain structures play a privileged role in the coming into existence of Christian reality. Just as structures such as magisterium and sacrament have been accepted as privileged channels of truth and grace (although this does not mean that there is no truth and grace apart from them, or even that the existence of the channels proves the reality of truth and grace), and conditions have therefore been set down for the exercise of the magisterium and the administration of the sacraments, so too it can be said that the Church of the poor is a structural channel for the coming into being of the true Church. Paraphrasing the terminology of sacramental theology, I might say that the Spirit is present in the poor *ex opere operato,* though this in no way means simply that with the poor as members the Church will come to exist as the authentic Church. What it does mean is that the Spirit manifests itself in the poor and that they are therefore structural channels for finding the truth of the Church and the direction and content of its mission.

The Church of the poor is not automatically the agent of truth and grace because the poor are in it; rather the poor in the Church are the structural source that assures the Church of being really the agent of truth and justice. In the final analysis, I am speaking of what Jesus refers to in Matthew 25 as the place where the Lord is to be found.

—*The True Church and the Poor, 91–95*

CHURCH OF THE POOR AS WELLSPRING OF KNOWLEDGE ABOUT JESUS CHRIST

In Latin America, realized faith in Christ accords a primacy to the moment of Christ's presence today in the poor. This is simply the classic theme of Matthew 25 taken seriously. That passage is useful not only for learning something about what Jesus has said, but for learning where he is presently to be found. . . .

But this realization of faith has two characteristic traits: the practice of liberation and the presence of Christ in the poor. . . . Both traits taken together specify the theologian's ecclesial *locus,* ineluctably, as the church of the poor.

In that church the totality of faith is . . . mediated by the liberative approach to the poor, as one recognizes Christ in them and corresponds to Christ in the approach to them. In this approach the poor actually evangelize those making the approach (see Puebla, no. 1147). This wellspring of theological cognition is supremely important for theologians and refers them more obviously to the historical Jesus.

Christology's ecclesial placement, accordingly, means one thing in Latin America and something different elsewhere. Ecclesial faith in Christ *de facto* exists . . . as a response to good news. That faith has two key elements: a liberative practice in conformity with the discipleship of Jesus and the encounter with Jesus in the poor, which requires an incarnation in the world of poverty. . . .

The "ecclesial placement" considered above is *de facto* accompanied by a determinate "social placement." The theologian reflects not only within the church but also within Latin America. This may appear evident, but it is not, for what is at stake is a placement within the *truth* of Latin America. It is difficult, as Paul warns us, to be in the truth of things, . . . and it is especially difficult to stay loyal to that truth and its exigencies. The truth of Latin America, furthermore, is a totality of multiple elements, which calls for a determination of which element or elements will contain a greater concentration of the total truth and afford a better access to the total truth.

A correct determination of this "partial" element of reality has not been easy for theology over the years and the centuries. It has actually been necessary for reality itself to manifest this element in what theology has termed the "sign of the times." "This sign is always the historically crucified people, who join to their permanency the ever distinct historical form of crucifixion," to which they are subjected in a given place and moment. To live in the crucified reality of Latin America, to accept it as it is and not attempt to disguise it in any way, is the first step in any process of theological cognition.

> If the state of domination and dependence in which two-thirds of humanity live, with an annual toll of thirty million dead from starvation and malnutrition, does not

become the starting point for *any* Christian theology today, even in the affluent and powerful countries, then theology cannot begin to relate meaningfully to the real situation.

These words of Hugo Assmann certainly apply to Latin America. If theology withdraws from this reality, it will have to listen to accusations of cynicism. But, even more important (where its epistemological condition is concerned): it will be accused of vacuity. "Its questions will lack *reality* and not relate to *real* men and women." The option "to go with the real," beginning with the flagrant situation of misery in Latin America, is a prerequisite for real cognition in the theological endeavor. The theologian's social placement, then, means being in that concrete, "partial" reality as the *locus* of access to the totality of Latin American reality and . . . its various elements.

> —"Ecclesial and Social Point of Departure of Latin American Christology," *Jesus in Latin America*, 61–62

"I HAVE CHOSEN AS MY STARTING POINT THE REALITY OF JESUS"

Let me say from the beginning that I have chosen as my starting point the reality of Jesus of Nazareth, his life, his mission and his fate, what is usually called the "historical Jesus." This is what I shall analyze in this chapter, but before that I shall explain the fundamental reasons for my choice in light of the serious difficulties it raised in relation of faith itself.

Jesus as the Way to Christ

Jesus Christ is a whole that, to put it for now in a simplified way, consists of a historical element (Jesus) and a transcendental element (Christ), and the most characteristic feature of faith as such is the acceptance of the transcendentral element: that this Jesus is more than Jesus, that he is *the* Christ. This acceptance is faith, which presupposed that Christ and the recognition of him are a gift of God, and that there is nothing that can force God to be like this or force us to recognize God mechanically as this . . . Given this, however, we cannot ignore two basic facts that make it possible and, in my opinion, very convenient, to start methodologically with the historical Jesus.

(i) God's descent into history cannot be understood . . . simply by accepting the great miracle and gift of this descent, but only when we examine what it really consists of. This reality is Jesus of Nazareth. In other words, it is not a matter simply of accepting in faith the miracle and the gift of God's having become a human being, but it is crucial to explain the detail of this process.

This divine miracle is nothing other than the real Jesus of Nazareth. Because of this, faith in Christ must be directed, also and essentially, from the outset to the underside of history, which in christology is indicated methodologically by the term "christology from below" or "ascending christology."

(ii) . . . Faith statements are . . . limit-statements, not directly accessible to human understanding. Calling them limit-statements does not mean that the things they talk about are meaningless, but it does mean that to have any knowledge of them, to be able to conceptualize and formulate them with a minimum of meaning, requires prior experience of historical realities, so that the ability to formulate and conceptualize these limit-realities presupposes a process that has to be gone through and only at the end of which will it be possible to maintain (or reject) such limit-statements.

This occurs in everyday life with phenomena such as love, freedom and life itself. And it occurs with theological phenomena. The statements that Jesus is Christ, that he is the expression of what is truly divine and truly human, are limit-statements, which, of their nature, require a process of understanding. That is not to say that undergoing this process automatically guarantees ultimate acceptance in faith of these limit-statements, but without this prior process what is confessed in faith would not have any describable meaning. Therefore in scripture transcendental limit-statements come preceded by historical statements. For example, in the canticle of Moses, God is referred to as essentially a liberator (a limit-statement), but this profession of faith comes preceded by the fact of the liberation from Egypt, attributed (in faith) to God. The fact of the liberation from Egypt—however historical it may be in all details—is something that can be known by reason, even if attributing it to God is a matter of faith. However, as regards the point that concerns us here, to make a meaningful limit-statement that God is a liberator, there must exist a prior phenomenon, liberation from Egypt.

The same happens with faith in Christ. To be able to confess meaningfully that Jesus is Christ, it is necessary to know Jesus, to know and analyze data about him which—though there is no obligation about this, since this leap is exclusively a matter of faith—enable a person to take the leap of faith and say, "Jesus is Christ."

This is clear from the formation of the first faith in Christ: the first believers were faced with many historical facts of Jesus' life and with the experience of the resurrection. And as a result of these experiences they started to think about who this Jesus was, until they eventually confessed him as Christ. This is true for the present as well, though not in the same way. In a sense, believers now have available to them the result of this process accomplished previously by others, faith in Christ. But it would be an illusion to think that here and now we can have direct access to the end of the process without going through (in life, of course, but also in thought) the stages that led to its formulation. This process began with Jesus of Nazareth. The logical process of christology is, therefore, chronological. Jesus can be understood as the way to Christ. —*Jesus the Liberator*, 36–37

THE *REALITY PRINCIPLE*: NEW TESTAMENT GUIDE TO THE HISTORICAL JESUS

In formal terms, the central presupposition of the christologies of the New Testament is what we might call the *reality principle*.

This means that the attributes, however egregious they may be (lord, exalted, word . . .), remain attributes, while the real and historical subject is still Jesus of Nazareth. Faith (and, indirectly, theology) is referred back to "what we have heard, what we have seen with our eyes, what we have looked at and touched with our hands" (1 Jn 1:1), although this, obviously, was to become analogous with the passage of time.

The New Testament builds its reflection on this reality of the historical Jesus and his resurrection. The patristic Age, on the other hand, became progressively removed not only from the historical Jesus . . . but also from the resurrection as a historical-eschatological event pointing to the end time, and it was increasingly to understand the reality of Christ from his historical origin (birth) and his transcendent origin (preexistence). . . .

It might be said that this process is inevitable and that we find ourselves in the same situation or worse, but this is not the case. Of course we cannot return to the actuality of Jesus, but we can take the reality principle seriously and decide on ways of allowing ourselves to be guided by it. Present-day christology, at least in Latin America, is conscious of this and tries to base itself on it. It does so by reevaluating the *reality* of Jesus of Nazareth, recalling it and understanding it as history. And it does so also by seeking his *actual presence*—said not purely metaphorically—in his body in history, above all in the martyrs and in the poor. This is not pure piety but theory: the crosses of history are a meditation on the cross of Jesus. And, importantly, through being real, they lead to its reality.

—*Christ the Liberator*, 225, 226, 228

MEANING OF "THE HISTORICAL JESUS"

Let us now examine what we mean . . . by the "historical Jesus" and what constitutes his positive value as a starting point for it.

(i) The most "historical" aspect of Jesus: practice with spirit. By "historical Jesus" we mean the life of Jesus of Nazareth, his

words and actions, his activity and his praxis, his attitudes and his spirit, his fate on the cross (and the resurrection). In other words, and expressed systematically, the history of Jesus.

Since this history is made up of many elements, we have to ask which of them is the "most historical," which is the best introduction to the whole reality of Jesus and best organizes the various elements of this whole . . .

My thesis is that the most historical aspect of the historical Jesus is his practice and the spirit with which he carried it out. By "practice" I mean the whole range of activities Jesus used to act on social reality and transform it in the specific direction of the Kingdom of God. The "historical" is thus primarily what sets history in motion, and this practice of Jesus', which in his day set history in motion, is what has come down to our time as a history set in motion to be continued.

The historical dimension of Jesus does not mean, therefore, from a formal point of view what is simply datable in space and time, but what is handed down to us as a trust for us to pass on in our turn. This implies treating the texts of the New Testament in general and the Gospel texts in particular as narratives published to keep alive through history a reality started off by Jesus. This reality, after the resurrection, is responsible for passing on faith in Christ, but in terms of Jesus' own intention its original task was to pass on his practice, in Jesus' own words, discipleship, considered primarily as a continuation of his practice. In this way, the community of perspectives required by hermeneutics is achieved in the continuance of Jesus' practice, which is necessary, though by no means sufficient, to understand the historical Jesus who initiated it. . . .

(ii) From the practice of Jesus to the "person" of Jesus. This formulation might be open to the objection that the "person" of Jesus disappears into his practice, with the result that we end up reproducing, on a different level, a serious error: just as Christ was reduced to an idea—something against which Personalist christology rightly fought—now we are reducing him to a

symbol for a style of action. The objection is serious, but it does not do justice to the facts.

(a) First and foremost, in the reality of faith as it is lived, the majority of Latin American Christians who follow the practice of Jesus—though there are always exceptions—do not abandon their faith in the person of Jesus. Very often quite the opposite happens: following the practice of Jesus leads them to a deeper faith in Jesus. . . . We go back to the practice of Jesus on the premise that this practice contains an essential element of *norma normans, non normata,* an absolute principle, not derived from anything else. . . . We have to go back to Jesus' practice, *because* it is Jesus'.

The essential content of this practice is the liberation of the oppressed, its approach is to . . . take on oneself the sin which is destroying them, its goal is the Kingdom of God, imbued with the spirit of the beatitudes. . . . In this sense, . . . Latin American christology wants Jesus' cause really to go on, but it is equally interested in the "Jesus" whose cause is to be advanced. This is both because it is interested in the whole Jesus and because, in order for Jesus' cause to go forward, it is very important to retrieve the "person" of Jesus.

(b) With this clarification, I think that Jesus' practice is what gives us the best chance of understanding and organizing all the elements that make him up: the events of his life, his teaching, his inner attitudes, his fate and his most intimate dimension, his person. I shall analyze this later in detail, but I want to look at it now in outline.

There can be no doubt that through Jesus' practice we understand better what he meant by Kingdom of God and anti-Kingdom, that his practice explains better than anything else his historical destiny on the cross and that it also helps us to understand his transcendent destiny, once we accept it in faith, his resurrection as God's justice to him. And his practice is also what enables us to sense the inner dimension of his person, his hope, his faith, his relationship with God. This is not to say that we can mechanically deduce from an analysis of his practice the sort of personal experience he had of God. . . . But the data we have are illuminated and enhanced by his practice, and the practice makes them coherent. In a word, I think that we have better access to the inner life of Jesus (his mind in history) from his outward practice (his making of history) than vice versa.

—"The Meaning of 'the Historical Dimension of Jesus' in Latin American Christology," *Jesus the Liberator*, 50–54

THE HISTORICAL JESUS AS REVELATION OF THE CHRISTIAN GOD

The writer who was most intellectually radical in arguing the need for and the importance of a return to the historical Jesus was Ignacio Ellacuría. His fundamental historical interest—"salvation history entails salvation in history" —led him to demand a new, "historically framed" reading of the "different christologies of the New Testament." The purpose is the following:

> Our new christology must give the history of the flesh-and-blood Jesus its full weight as revelation. Today it would be absolutely ridiculous to try to fashion a christology in which the historical realization of Jesus' life did not play a decisive role. The "mysteries of Jesus' life," which once were treated peripherally as part of ascetics, must be given their full import—provided, of course, that we explore exegetically and historically what the life of Jesus really was.

In epistemological terms, "We have to move on to a historical *logos*, without which every other *logos* is merely speculative and idealist." In theological terms, "The historical life of Jesus is the fullest revelation of the Christian God."

The original, insight of the theology of liberation is thus very clear: "We must go back to Jesus." Without his specific historicity, Christ becomes an icon. —*Jesus the Liberator*, 46–47

WHAT KARL RAHNER HAS MEANT FOR ME

"If at all possible, we needed to Salvadorize Rahner"

I must confess that until 1974, when I returned to El Salvador, the world of the poor—that is, the real world—did not exist for me. . . . We had to awaken from the dream. Awakening was painful and wrenching in my case; it was as if layers of skin were being removed one by one. Fortunately, there was light as well as darkness in the awakening. Karl Rahner's theology—I mention him because he was for me the one who left the most lasting and beneficial impression—was my companion during those years, and his pages on the mystery of God continue to accompany me even today. . . .

But from the beginning it became quite clear that truth, love, faith, the gospel of Jesus, God, the very best we have as people of faith and as human beings—these were somehow to be found among the poor and in the cause of justice. I do not mean to imply that Rahner and Jürgen Moltmann, whom I studied avidly, no longer had anything to say to me. But I did come to understand that it was absurd to go about trying to Rahnerize or Moltmannize the people of El Salvador. If there was something positive I could bring from the perspective of my studies, the task would have to be the reverse: If at all possible, we needed to Salvadorize Rahner and Moltmann.   —*The Principle of Mercy*, 2–3

"Ellacuría was not just Rahner's pupil; he took forward important ideas . . . in his own historical situation"

During the 1970s, a new church and a new theology arose in Latin America. This article is a personal reflection on what Karl Rahner has meant for me in that context, though I hope that what I say will apply to liberation theology more broadly. I write out of the life-experience in El Salvador that has led me to read with new eyes the theology I had previously studied, in which Rahner's work was a very important element. I am also writing out of my close personal and intellectual relationship with Ignacio Ellacuría, Rahner's student in Innsbruck between 1958 and

1962. On account of his defense of faith and justice, Ellacuría, as many will know, was murdered on 16 November 1989, along with five other Jesuits and two female workers from the university in which he taught. But we should remember that Ellacuría was not just Rahner's pupil. He took forward important ideas in Rahner's theology, as he sought to express them in his own historical situation and in a way appropriate for the world of the poor. This . . . shall try to explore Rahner's influence on liberation theology. . . .

Rahner's Influence on Liberation Theology

To set out Rahner's influence on liberation theology inevitably involves oversimplification. It was Rahner's dogmatic theology, rather than his philosophy, that was crucial in this connection. And we must remember that there are many different liberation theologies, even in Latin America. His influence was probably unconscious and unintentional, enabling liberation theologians to develop approaches that were new, and distinctively Latin American. Of this I am convinced, though it is no easy task to specify just what form Rahner's contribution took.

For me, Rahner's contribution to liberation theology centered on the fundamental attitude with which he undertook the theological task, the existential disposition with which he set about making theological sense of reality. Rahner had no special insight into realities central for the new theology such as the liberation of the poor, but his way of approaching God through reflection on human reality, and of approaching human reality through reflection on God, greatly benefited liberation theology at its origins. Let me simply mention some aspects of what I mean.

Theology and Reality

What struck me in Rahner's theology was how reality itself was its foundation. The point may seem obvious, but there are theologies that start from preconceived notions in which this principle is not often observed. Be that as it may, Rahner was outstanding in his fidelity to the real.

In his well-known article on the theology of the symbol, Rahner wrote of how all realities were symbolic because they "necessarily 'express' themselves in order to attain their own nature."[5] Perhaps I am overstating the point, but I think that Rahner's theology can be understood as a service to this process. Rahner was able to convey a taste for lived reality. In Latin, the words for *taste* and *wisdom* are connected, and Rahner was, in the root sense of the word, a sapiential thinker. . . .

And remember, too, how his first big article reacted against the conventional tradition with the plaintive "it can't be like this."[6] Rahner would think, ruminate, argue—but the process ended not with a conclusion arrived at through logical steps, nor with the rounding off of a rational argument, but rather with proclamation of the reality that was expressing itself.

Mutatis mutandis, I believe that the foundational moments of liberation theology were also marked by this insistence on placing reality at the center of thinking. Liberation theology did not begin with concepts or sophisticated arguments, but with reality. In Ignatian language, it discovered its "principle and foundation" in this reality, the in-breaking of the poor, and stayed close to this foundational reality amid all the theorizing.

To put the point more graphically: liberation theology's fundamental assertion and conviction is that the poor—and God in the poor— have broken into history. The believer, the human person, has to respond to this reality, indeed correspond to it. We are charged to liberate the poor and, in Ellacuría's phrase, to take them down from their cross. Theology can no longer be the ideology that fosters oppression. None of these convictions is just the result of a theoretical argument; they come from an honest and hopeful option to let lived reality be central, to let

---

5. Rahner, "The Theology of the Symbol," 224.
6. Rahner, "Remarks on the Theological Treatise de Trinitate," 87.

it speak, to hear its word, to let it guide us and call forth our response.

A further scandalous and novel step—though one seen more in liberation theology than in Rahner—is the recognition that salvation lies precisely in these poor people. They are sustaining us; they are enlightening us about God and about ourselves; in some undeserved and unexpected way, they are keeping our hope alive. Liberation theology does not conclude all this from the ideas it had before (though it was certainly schooled in older theologies); rather it discovers and extends what it finds as it engages lived reality. "The glory of God is the poor person who is alive." "You—who are poor and who are victims— are the suffering servant of God for today, the crucified people." "The poor are evangelizing us." These pithy phrases, from Archbishop Romero, from Ellacuría, from the Puebla assembly, proclaim what is actually happening. They match Rahner for radicality and frankness.

Reality as Mystery

This reality has a mystery at its heart. God is the mystery par excellence, and the human person is the being confronted with mystery. Rahner insists that God is the *Holy* Mystery who, without ceasing to be mystery, is essentially salvific—no longer is there any question of God's either saving or condemning us. This conviction runs right into the details of Rahner's Christology and ecclesiology. Thus the Church of this God, by virtue of its affinity with God, can canonize, pronounce where absolute salvation can be found. But it cannot condemn; it cannot make a similar pronouncement about damnation.

Rahner has a deeper sense of God's mystery than other standard progressive theologians, one that is matched in liberation theology. Gutiérrez places mystery, God's mystery, at the center. Without being artificial, I believe the liberation theology understands the poor person as mystery: not just a particular case that makes ethical demands, nor even just as a person who might be saved, but rather as a *reality freighted with the Mystery*.

The inbreaking of the poor person, and of God within them, recalls much of Rahner's account of mystery. The poor person is the Other who is distant, who cannot be manipulated; because they have been oppressed, they are different and demanding. But at the same time they are the Other who is close, saving, the Holy Mystery. Thus Ellacuría could write of the crucified people as the presence of the mystery of God, and regard this presence as itself saving. As is too little known, he spoke of a soteriology of history.[7]

Reality and the Sacramental

One point on which Rahner was insistent was that reality is intrinsically symbolic: it seeks to express itself. It is well known that Rahner, along with others such as Otto Semmelroth, developed an understanding of the Church as itself sacramental, and of the seven sacraments as an expression of this primordial sacramentality.[8] But all this is grounded in the sacramentality of Jesus. Let it suffice to recall Rahner's brilliant interpretation of the Incarnation: when God became human, Christ's flesh (*sarx*) was not a mere livery; it was, simply and radically, the manifestation of the divine in our world.[9] On this basis, Rahner could speak of the eternal significance of Jesus' humanity for our relationship with God. Ellacuría used to add, by way of commentary, that this world was a world of sin: becoming flesh was not just a metaphysical descent, but rather an immersion in a deathly historical reality.

Though liberation theology has not developed a theory of the sacraments, the idea of the Church as primordial sacrament is certainly present within it. The central conviction of liberation theology is that of God's presence in the poor. This implies that mysticism and politics, the transcendent and the historical, can and must converge. Thus liberation theology takes human history

---

7. Ellacuría, "The Crucified People," 580–603.
8. Rahner, *The Church and the Sacraments*.
9. Rahner, "The Theology of the Symbol," 237–40.

with absolute seriousness—it may be distinguishable from the reality of God, but it may not be separated from the reality of God, still less set in opposition to it. The vulgar criticisms of liberation theology, to the effect that it is sociology rather than theology, simply miss the point that history expresses God, is sacramentally charged with God. And as the crucified people represent the second Isaiah's Servant, they too are a sacrament of God.

Transcendence here is not something beyond history but within it. The history of God and of humanity becomes one single "great history of God." Rahner had begun to deal with this theme in an important article, "History of the World and Salvation History,"[10] and his idea of grace present in all human existence, the so-called supernatural existential, also contributed. What we call the problem of nature and grace is in reality the question of there being one single history, always graced by God, but with a grace that human freedom can reject. Liberation theology insists that there is only one history, with two dimensions that we need to see as a history of grace and a history of sin—abstract distinctions like "nature and grace" or "sacred and secular" will not do.

The Logic of Lived Experience

If we move now to the quality of Rahner's engagement with reality, we can begin with Rahner's conviction that God, God's own self and God's will, can be and is given to us in what simply happens, in ways that nothing else can specify or predict. Moreover, such happenings can be recognized as coming from God. . . . We need to respond to the specific happenings, needs and desires that are "true signs of God's presence and purpose" [*Gaudium et spes*, n. 11].

This sense of God's active presence in history to be discerned through the signs of the times, and of the will of God not being reducible to universal principles, is also central to the theology

---

10. Rahner, *Theological Investigations 5*, 97–114.

of liberation. From the beginning, Gutiérrez' fundamental conviction has been that the poor are not just objects of our consideration and benevolent options. Rather the poor, with their sufferings and hopes, have "broken into" history, irrupted into it.[11] Moreover, God has broken in with the poor, and people have been able to receive that inbreaking in a way that does not amount simply to a deduction from what they already knew. Once it has occurred . . . the basic reception of the irruption . . . emerges from the dependence on experience that is characteristic of human ("the poor have broken in") and religious ("and God within them") logic. Within conventional theology prior to Rahner, these statements of liberation theology would have been quite impossible, but Rahner's own theology both grounds and echoes them.

Theology Leading into Mystery

For Rahner, the fact that God is Mystery leads to a conception of theology as leading into mystery. All theological realities can and should be referred to God, the one and only Mystery, from whom they derive their significance and intelligibility.

Personally, I believe that in liberation theology, the place of the poor is similar. Though facile parallels must be avoided, it nevertheless follows that if God is present in the poor person, then we must be able to use the same logic in talking about the poor that we use regarding God. With all due caution, I do believe that liberation theology can legitimately speak of the poor person as an ultimate, and of the option for the poor as defining my identity—what I can know, what I have to do, what I can rightly hope for and celebrate. Theology can amount to a *reductio in pauperes*, a process of leading us into the mystery which is poor.

It follows that theology can talk of the Church—without doing violence to the faith or manipulating the poor—as essentially a Church of the poor. It can speak of how the poor

---

11. Gutiérrez, *The Power of the Poor in History*.

have a potential for evangelization, . . . working—in Ellacuría's phrase—to take the crucified people down from their cross. And on the last day, they will be our judges. John Paul II put the point sharply in Canada in 1985: "the poor countries will judge the rich ones." But, in my experience in El Salvador, one often has to add that the poor will also pardon us, an experience which brings home to me the truth of Rahner's saying that you know you are a sinner only if you are pardoned. . . .

Theology and Spirituality

For Rahner, theology is not just a matter of knowledge and practice but also of spirituality:

> In my theology what is of fundamental significance for me is the givenness of a genuine, primordial experience of God and of God's Spirit. This is logically (though not necessarily chronologically) prior to reflection and to theological verbalization, and it can never be fully appropriated by reflection.[12]

Rahner is making not only a personal claim but also a methodological one. The experience of God is both the source and the goal of his theology. His use of a particular intellectual tool, transcendental thought, is secondary.

Liberation theology, too, takes commitment and experience as foundational. From the very beginning, liberation theologians have insisted that their theology is a secondary outgrowth, and that what is primary is an experience of faith and a praxis of liberation; our theology is our spirituality.[13] . . .

Differences

I have been noting the fundamental influence of Rahner on liberation theology. This is rarely an influence at the level of content,

---

12. *Karl Rahner in Dialogue: Conversations and Interviews 1965–1982*, 328.

13. For example, Gutiérrez, "Speaking about God," 27–31.

even though liberation theologians accepted many of Rahner's ideas. Nor did Rahner have any direct influence on what was most specific to the theology of liberation: the idea of liberation coming from the poor, and the impact this would have on our ways of conceiving God, Christ and the Church. Rahner's contribution was a significant one, but it was indirect.

As liberation theology came to birth, it found inspiration and theological legitimation in Rahner's general approach to theology, even though he did not speak of liberation, and in his handling of the theologies with which he took issue. The influence operated principally at the level of what I would call "theological attitude." It encouraged creativity, freedom, responsibility both to history and to the contemporary world, and gospel-centeredness. By this last I mean taking Jesus as the unconditional norm for interpreting important realities and not the other way round. At this attitudinal level, there was certainly a convergence between Rahner and the liberation theologians.

Obviously there were some significant differences. Rahner engaged the Enlightenment as represented by Kant; liberation theology engaged the Enlightenment as represented by Marx. What they shared was a concern to take the challenges utterly seriously.

Moreover, liberation theology would now see important gaps in Rahner's theology. He did not offer any analysis of praxis as a dimension of human knowledge; he did not present salvation as a liberative reality in history. More surprisingly, his brilliant retrieval of the humanity of Christ did not explore the cross fully. In his final period he may have become more sensitive to the realities of the world, but he did not develop a theological method appropriate to them. We could not call Rahner's theology prophetic, even if, right up to the end of his life, his theology did express the utopian vision of Christianity. Metz tells us that he would reproach Rahner for theologizing without reckoning with Auschwitz. And I do not think Rahner ever came to understand Ellacuría's utopian conception of a "civilization of poverty" in contrast to the "civilization of wealth" that has never given life or dignity to its minorities.[14] Yet this vision has deep gospel roots, and, in the meditation on Two Standards, Ignatian ones.

Rahner could have dealt with themes of this kind, but they came too late for him. Nevertheless, we should not forget his support for the Church and the way of Christian life that was emerging in Latin America in his last years. As a human being and a theologian, Rahner was moving in his last years towards what was best in liberation theology, and he would have made his own contribution towards it, at once critical and stimulating.

Lost in the Mystery of God

Let me end more personally. My own first encounter with Rahner was through his little book *On the Theology of Death*, which I came across by chance when I was a student in St. Louis in the 1960s. I later read and studied many other things that he wrote, but I never forgot this remarkable book on death. Let me recall two points from this book that are fundamentals here in El Salvador, points on which, to use a classic term, the Church stands or falls.

Firstly, Rahner says that martyrdom is "the Christian death par excellence."[15] How often that phrase has come back to me in El Salvador! Whether something from Rahner's personal experience lies in the background, or whether this is just another of his profound dogmatic statements, I do not know. . . .

Secondly, there was Rahner's vision of death. As he put it in the interview quoted at the very beginning of this article: "The true summit of my life has yet to arrive. I mean the abyss which is the mystery of God, into which we hurl ourselves with the hope of being accepted by His love and His mercy."[16]

"Summit," "yet to arrive," "mystery of God," "to be accepted by His love and His mercy." Is there a liberation theology here?

---

14. Ellacuría, "Utopia and Prophecy in Latin America," 289–328.

15. Rahner, *On the Theology of Death*, 109.

16. Rahner, *Faith in a Wintry Season*, 38.

The answer to that question is not so important. But I like what Pedro Casaldáliga, Christian, bishop and poet of liberation, wrote after Rahner's death:

> "What are you doing now?"
> the Pope used to ask him (inquisitorially? kindly?).
> The theologian used to reply (evasively? magisterially?),
> "I am preparing to live the great Encounter."
> And with eighty Aprils, well-pondered,
> a hearer of the Mystery in the Word,
> he plunged into the absolute future.[17]
> —"Karl Rahner and Liberation Theology," 53–66.

JESUS, SACRAMENT OF GOD, REAL SYMBOL OF THE WORD

Karl Rahner's Speculative Explanation

Let us now make a short excursus into Rahner's thesis on the unity of divinity and humanity in Jesus Christ, a true and deep expression of holistic reality. Its originality lies in two things: the first, in understanding humanity with essential reference to divinity; the second, in understanding the relationship between both elements according to a sacramental theoretical model, so that Jesus is the sacrament of God and humanity is the sacrament of divinity. I shall develop the first point later. On the second, I should say that, speculatively, Rahner is trying to explain how the *sarx* of John 1:14 is the real symbol of the Word and is so to such an extent—he adds—that "if I had to write a theology of symbolic reality, christology, as the doctrine of the incarnation of the Word, would, clearly, have to form the pivotal chapter," and its development would revolve around this unique phrase: "Whoever has seen me has seen the Father" (Jn 14:9). . . .

Jesus, Real Symbol of the Word

This overall reality cannot, obviously, be understood as mere coexistence or juxtaposition of two things. Seeking an adequate

---

17. Casaldáliga, "Salmo de abril en Sao Paulo," 39.

theoretical expression for it, Rahner uses the sacramentality of the real: the human, Jesus, is the real symbol of the Word—by which false or inadequate interpretations are left behind. The basic error would consist in viewing human nature as the previous element, given and known before the incarnation, since in this case human nature would be seen as a uniform, which would indicate God but not be his real symbol; it would be an arbitrary sign, put on from outside, which really *does not* manifest God, even if by God's positive decree this human nature referred back to God. Neither can nature be seen as an instrument manipulated by God from the outside but without telling us who God is. It is not strange—Rahner added, writing forty years ago—, that when such suppositions are implicitly or explicitly present in a christology Christ is revealing the Father through his *teaching* or through his *powerful* actions but not through what he is.

Refusing to understand the unity of the divine and the human in Jesus Christ as subsequent, that is, as the union of two realities that—even if only logically—could exist independently of one another[,] is still more grave. The Word did not take on a human nature already constituted logically; he took on human nature in creating it and created it in taking it on; he took it on in alienating himself. The humanity of Christ is, then, that created reality which becomes the Word when the Word alienates itself, goes outward from itself. And this human nature remains the symbol of the Word for always, including in the beatific vision. "The eternal significance of the humanity of Jesus for our relationship with God" does no more than affirm that since the incarnation the human Jesus is the real symbol of God and that therefore—not being provisional and transitory but a real symbol—he is the mediator for all eternity.

Jesus Christ and the Unification of Human Beings

. . . Ultimately, Rahner is stating that humanity—with the necessary qualifications—can come to be in fundamental union with God. Chalcedon is then a fundamentally holistic definition.

We can perhaps reach a similar conclusion through an anthropology of biblical stamp. —*Christ the Liberator*, 317, 319, 320

A PROCESS OF UNDERSTANDING THAT BEGINS WITH THE HUMAN REALITY OF JESUS

A Specific Epistemology

I said in chapter 6 that statements about God in himself are possible only through a *process* of understanding. . . .

The process begins with *the human reality of Jesus,* which in principle is historically verifiable. That his being is truly human was demonstrated in the previous volume. . . . Summarily, we can say that, in his life, Jesus refers to God without God "de-humanizing" him, and so to the end, despite crisis, agony, and death. (What happens to the divinity in Jesus' life is not verifiable but can only be inferred and believed. But, once accepted in a later faith, we could and should say that in Jesus of Nazareth God comes close to humanity, without this humanity "de-divinizing" God, although it does actualize God to a scandalous extent.)

The human reality, now approached through faith, is *placed in relationship with God.* This is what New Testament and patristic christological reflection do in various ways, as we have seen in earlier chapters, through titles and theological interpretations of his life. The outcome is to establish a special relationship between Jesus and God.

The process *ends with confessing the divinity of Jesus Christ in* himself, which incipiently in the New Testament and explicitly after Nicaea, come about through surrendering reason to mystery. . . .

For epistemology, what matters is the conclusion: understanding the reality of Jesus-Christ-in-himself can be achieved only through . . . a process of understanding that begins in the New Testament and, within that, in the texts that deal with the actual life and fate of Jesus, to which were added—later—the theological interpretations the New Testament and the Fathers of the church made of these. And they end in the surrender of reason to mystery.

This epistemology includes, then, two essential elements: the way of understanding, which begins with some reality of a historical-nature, and the *surrender* of reason at the end of the process. These two elements—way and surrender—are what I want to look at now, not only in their theoretical cognitive dimension but also in their working historical reality.

—*Christ the Liberator,* 321–23

FOLLOWING THE HISTORICAL JESUS AS *MYSTAGOGIA*[18]

Through the presentation of the historical Jesus and of the most historical aspects of Jesus, Latin American christology seeks personal access to Jesus. It does this, not by presenting primarily items of knowledge about him . . ., but by presenting his practice so that it can be recreated and so give access to Jesus. . . . To follow the practice of Jesus with his spirit is an ethical demand of the historical Jesus himself, but it is also an epistemological principle. I said earlier that knowledge of a limit-phenomenon requires knowledge of objective prior historical phenomena, and now I am saying that . . . in the case of faith in Christ, the prior objective phenomenon . . . is . . . the historical Jesus and the prior subjective experience is being his disciple.

To put it negatively, outside discipleship we cannot have sufficient affinity with the object of faith to know what we are talking about when we confess Jesus as the Christ. Positively, through the affinity produced by discipleship it can be meaningful to proclaim Jesus as Christ, as the revelation of true divinity and true humanity. In the language of the New Testament, it is God's plan that we should become "children in the Son," . . . and . . . by becoming sons and daughters we attain affinity with the Son and can come to know him.

---

18. The Catechism of the Catholic Church defines *mystagogy* as initiation "into the mystery of Christ by proceeding from the visible to the invisible, from the sign to the thing signified, from the 'sacraments' to the 'mysteries.'" *Catechism,* #1075.

Discipleship as Mystagogia

In this section I have argued, essentially, that by starting from the historical Jesus and the most historical aspect of Jesus: Latin American christology seeks to be christology in the strict sense. On the level of method—although the real faith of believers and of theologians includes from the beginning some sort of overall faith in Christ—it considers that the logical path of christology is basically chronological. This appears in the following form in the New Testament: (a) the mission of Jesus in the service of the Kingdom, that is, his practice and the demand to engage in it, (b) the mystery of Jesus' identity and (c) the confession of his unrepeatable and saving reality, faith in Christ.

Twenty centuries later we have inherited what one might call the completed process of christology. As a result the *real* starting point is always, in one way, overall faith in Christ, but the *methodological* starting point continues to be the historical Jesus. This is, objectively the best *mystagogia* for gaining access to Jesus and so to Christ.   —*Jesus the Liberator, 55*

THE REIGN OF GOD: CENTER
OF JESUS' LIFE

Years ago a "Copernican" change occurred in my thinking when I realized that the Reign of God was at the center of Jesus' life— both the "Reign" and "God." I wrote at that time that "Jesus did not preach about himself, or just about God, but rather he preached about the Reign of God." The point is that his reality was ex-centric (or other-centered), and that this is fundamental to the Jesus approach. The Church must therefore take this into account in "speaking about Jesus," and it should reproduce this ex-centricity in its "sending on mission." To negate this *in actu* by putting itself at the center of its own preaching is to vitiate its essence at the roots. This is a recurring temptation into which the Church repeatedly falls. And it makes it difficult—outside of miracles of grace—for the mission to be efficacious.

The Reign Must Be Announced and Initiated

. . . In order to pursue mission following Jesus' approach, the Church must put itself clearly at the service of the Reign, overcoming the temptation to put itself at the center. It should incarnate itself in history in what makes the Reign grow or diminish, where it should *promote grace* and work to *eradicate sin*. It should do this with *solidarity*, making its own "the joys and hopes, the sorrows and the sufferings of all, especially the poor and those who suffer." And it must do this *seriously*: for sin is *trivialized* and salvation *vanishes* when the Reign of God is not taken seriously.

Additionally, like Jesus, we must remember the reality of the anti-Reign when speaking about mission. We should take responsibility for it, combat it, and be ready to suffer the consequences. We must get in tune with the God of the Reign, and above all with his *mercy* toward the oppressed, but also with his *anger*, which is most often forgotten: "Woe to those who sell the needy for a pair of sandals!" said Amos (Amos 2:6c). "Woe to you who tie up heavy burdens, and who kill the prophets," said Jesus (Matthew 23: 4, 30–31).

This prophetic approach is essential for mission. The Church's social teaching and ethics are good, but as good as they are, they are not enough. A thunderous prophecy is needed. And the final reason for the Church is that it must denounce *idolatry*, not in the form of the sterile tautology, "nothing created should be absolutized," a denunciation that doesn't bother anybody, but rather as denunciation of what idolatry truly is: a cult of idols, realities that are very real. That is how Archbishop Romero expressed it, which he explained very well in his fourth pastoral letter in 1979. Idols are historical existential realities, they promise salvation, they demand orthodoxy and a cult, and they require victims in order to survive, like the god Moloch. Archbishop Romero denounced the absolutization of capital and national security as idols, as Puebla also did (#493–497,

498–506), and he denounced the absolutization of popular organizations, which are good in themselves, but which become idols when they demand endless victims.

On the Continent these idols who demand victims continue to exist. Yet there is a shortage of condemnations from the Church about such an important matter. The reason is understandable: confronting the idols automatically brings conflict, and so it is avoided. Additionally, we create ideologies legitimating a false peace and being on good terms with everybody, sometimes even those who favor the anti-Reign, so that we can do all this with a clean conscience. But a mission following the approach of Jesus must take the idols into account, analyzing them deeply and combating them without deceiving ourselves. Short of this, we are lacking something fundamental from the approach of Jesus. Building the Reign and struggling against the anti-Reign is an essential task, and it is what gives "weight" to the mission of the Church. Without it, mission is simply carried away by the wind.

—Address by Jon Sobrino on the 19th anniversary of the UCA martyrs;
translated by Lassalle-Klein in *Jesus of Galilee*, 90, 92, 93

CORRESPONDENCE BETWEEN THE REALITIES OF JESUS AND HIS FOLLOWERS IN EL SALVADOR

This article, published soon after the criticisms by the Congregation for the Doctrine of the Faith, responds indirectly to the accusation that "the 'Church of the poor' assumes the fundamental position that properly belongs to the faith of the Church."[19] *Sobrino's response is that, in accepting the normative faith of the church about Jesus Christ, he is called to explore "correspondences" between the historical reality of Jesus and the contemporary situation of the church in El Salvador. Sobrino's response illustrates his notion that spirituality should be understood as the relationship of the spirit of the subject to the*

---

19. Congregation for the Doctrine of the Faith, *Notification*, I/2.

historical reality in which she/he lives (see "Foundations of Spirituality" in Chapter 4). He enumerates three correspondences: (1) the historical reality of Galilee and the historical reality of El Salvador, (2) the persecution of Jesus and that of the Salvadoran martyrs, and (3) the paschal mystery lived both by Jesus and the crucified people of El Salvador, understood as the Suffering Servant of Yahweh who brings salvation.

In this article I want to show how the Gospels' *text* about Jesus has been read in the Salvadoran *context*—which stands as a symbol of a much larger Third World. . . . In what follows I will . . . focus on three things. First, simply put, there exists a certain *correspondence* between the reality of Galilee then and our reality in the Third World today. Second, during the 1970s *reality broke in,* and made itself deeply felt. Third, there occurred a powerful *epistemological rupture* in the functioning of intelligence in Salvadoran reality, though this rupture was not exclusive to that context.

Correspondence between the Reality That Appears in the Text and in the Context

Correspondence of the Social Realities of Galilee and El Salvador

In terms of a *location* from which the sources are being read, I understand El Salvador not just as a special reality, an *ubi*, nor simply as a cultural reality (although one must take this into account as an important element, especially in the neighboring indigenous world of Guatemala), but rather above all as a substantial *quid.* The essential elements of this reality are poverty, injustice, structural oppression and repression, and slow violent death. These elements also include clinging to life (humanly and religiously) and hope for the liberation of the majorities who, though innocent and substantially undefended, have been slowly and violently rewarded with death. This is historically evident, and it is critical to take it into account, if not in the details at least in substance, if one is to understand the Galilee of Jesus. The reality of El Salvador helps one understand Jesus' Galilee. The nature of Galilee's historical sin and grace is better understood through the *real* sin and grace of El Salvador, not only our thoughts *about* that sin and grace.

Correspondence among the Bearers of Salvation: Jesus and the Salvadoran Martyrs

It is important to emphasize another form of correspondence, however, one that is almost never taken into account, even though it should be carefully considered. In El Salvador—a Third World country not normally considered a part of the world of abundance, certainly not with regard to martyrdom—many human beings, despite suffering greater or lesser poverty or austerity, live, like Jesus, with unconditional mercy, defending the poor and the victims produced by very real economic, military, political, cultural, media, and imperial gods. They do this in fidelity to God with integrity *to the very end*, and with a love that makes them willing to give their lives. These are the martyrs. And Jesus is well pleased to call them *brothers and sisters*.

These men and women provide a privileged place from which to reread the texts about Jesus of Galilee and to better understand his life, praxis, and destiny. They even shed light on the *pro me* of Jesus, so beloved by Paul and Ignatius of Loyola, though the *pro me* must be historicized from the *pro pauperibus*.

The poor also help us get to know, or at least guess at, Jesus' filial relationship with a God who is a Father in whom one can trust, and with a Father who continues being a God to whom one must always remain available for service. I cannot expand on this point here, but it is important, since Christologies usually squeeze out an inadequate treatment of the relationship of Jesus to God in favor of the relationship of Jesus to the kingdom of God. Nonetheless, the Salvadoran context illuminates the relationship of Jesus to God, certainly in quality if not in quantity. One has only to mention the names of Archbishop Oscar Romero and Rutilio Grande, S.J. They not only resemble Jesus the *evangelizer and prophet*, but also Jesus, the *Son* of God.

We must also remember the theological dimension of this correspondence. Jesus "went about doing good, for God was with him" (Acts 10:38b), said Peter in the house of Cornelius. So too, three days after Archbishop Romero's assassination, Ellacuría said in a homily at the University of Central America, "With Archbishop Romero, God visited El Salvador."[20] Once again, then, given all the required qualifications, we cannot ignore the fundamental correspondence of these events with the journey of Jesus through history.

Global Correspondence of Oppression and Repression

Readers who inhabit contexts far from ours may obviously conclude that, as El Salvador is not his or her context, the christology emerging from here is not straightforwardly transferable. But things are not so simple, for the context I have described is not an esoteric exception or an unimportant anecdote to the story of the planet today. Indeed, the truth is quite the opposite. What is esoteric is the world of prosperity, not the world of El Salvador.

If one goes to the real foundation of our world—which is a jealously guarded secret—one discovers a fundamental correspondence between the Galilee of Jesus and the many other galilees of our world, a world of those who are poor and victims. This world structurally reproduces what occurred in the Roman Empire, under which Galilee lived.

Trying to make the language of *empire* disappear is a cover-up. And it is self-interested euphemism to substitute the language of *globalization*, which is also deceptive since the term "globe" is close to "sphere," suggesting a "perfection" that is absolutely nonexistent in the terrestrial globe today. And we must not forget the fundamental reality of the *imperium magnum latrocinium* (great thieving empire), as Augustine called it, which yesterday was Rome and today is life under the aegis of the United States. This larceny is the ground of the correspondence of which I speak, exposing both its existence and its cruelty. The *pax romana* was cruel. Today UN expert Jean Ziegler says that the world of plenty is an assassin: "'Every child who

---

20. Ignacio Ellacuría, *Escritos teológicos*, 4 vols. (San Salvador: UCA, 2002–2002) 3:93–100.

dies from hunger is assassinated' because it could have been prevented."[21]

This is the dominant correspondence from the perspective of sin. However, this correspondence can also be seen *sub specie contrarii*, i.e., from the perspective of grace: the hope of the Galilee of Jesus; the many movements in which his hope was expressed; the incipiently liberating praxis; and finally utopia: the life blood of the poor. It is enough for the moment to mention it.

Global Correspondence of Martyrs Like Jesus

The correspondence of those who bring salvation is also global. There have been movements of life and liberation in many places, and, above all, an immense collection of martyrs on which I will focus now. Limiting myself to El Salvador and Guatemala, two well-known bishops, Romero and Juan José Gerardi (plus a third in El Salvador, Joaquín Ramos, who is less well known), around thirty priests, and a dozen religious have been assassinated. There is also an interminable list of catechists, delegates of the Word, workers for nongovernmental organizations, and solidarity groups that began their work long before they began to officially exist as such. They did their work without administrative apparatus, with only the light of the Gospel and a bit of enlightenment contributed by the theology of liberation, sometimes with rudiments of Marxism, with limitless generosity, and with a *parresía* for speaking the truth and denouncing the horrors of oppression and repression. They are the glory of the people and of many churches, not only in El Salvador and Guatemala but the entire Third World—for example, Archbishop Christophe Munaihirwa of Bukavu, Congo, assassinated in 1996 for defending hundreds of thousands of refugees in Rwanda; today he is called "the Romero of Africa."

---

21. United Nations, "Press Conference by United Nations Special Rapporteur on Right to Food," October 26, 2007. https://www.un.org/press/en/2007/071026_Ziegler.doc.htm.

Jesus-like martyrdom is neither esoteric nor exceptional on the world stage.

Correspondence of Faith: The Crucified People, Suffering Servant of Yahweh

To the above-named correspondence I must add another that extends throughout the Third World: *the analogical correspondence of the poor and victims of today with the Suffering Servant who carries the sin of the world, ransoms, and saves us.* While this correspondence is more difficult to specify factually because it is perceptible only from a faith-based interpretation of the texts, nevertheless, this is how we have seen the Suffering Servant in El Salvador. Referring to the poor and the victims as "the crucified people" and "the pierced divinity," Archbishop Romero and Ignacio Ellacuría have described them as a historical sacrament of the Suffering Servant. At the descriptive level the Servant Songs of Isaiah and Passion Narratives of the Gospels correspond with what is happening in our world today, and vice versa. The originality of this idea, however, lies not in asserting this correspondence but in conceding dignity to the victims of today: there is something sacred about them. The greatest innovation, however, has been to consider them bearers of salvation. In this above all they converge with the Servant who takes away the sin of the world, and, scandalously, brings salvation.

There are hundreds of millions of poor and oppressed in the world, in whom appears what I have called "primordial holiness," seen in their untiring clinging to life, one to another in repressions, wars, migrations, and refugee centers. Miraculously many times they remain hopeful, offer pardon, and search for reconciliation. Moreover, they have a convening power, which generates solidarity, understood as mutual support, giving to one another and receiving one another with the best that one has. Those who come from the world of plenty to help the poor repeatedly say, with thanks, that they have received more than they have given. Therefore, looking at both the world of abundance and the world of poverty, I have said *extra pauperes nulla salus* (outside the poor there is no salvation). Taking one step further, salvation comes from the poor. They are the servant of Yahweh.

The Servant and the Crucified One help us understand the poor and the victims of our context. This does not imply that I think it is possible to turn to reflection without falling into oversimplifications, because the victims do not make us almost mechanically and entirely understand the figure of Jesus. His everyday life was not like that of the majorities of the poor and oppressed of our world. But they can certainly help us understand the significance of his life and destiny. We accept in faith that Jesus is the Servant who brings salvation. But understanding—with all the required qualifications—that today's victims can bring salvation allows one also to understand, a bit, what it is about Jesus of Nazareth and his destiny that brings salvation.

The conclusion, then, is that El Salvador (the Congo, Haiti, Bangladesh), and not the world of abundance (Washington, Paris, Madrid), offers a correspondence with the Galilee of Jesus and with Jesus of Galilee. The crucified people bear the sin of the world and redeem it, saving us.

The Irruption of Reality

The correspondence I have analyzed is finally based in poverty, yesterday and today. It has existed for centuries, but neither the poverty that appears in the Gospel *text*, much less the Salvadoran *context*, has been taken into account in christology. Since the end of the 1970s, however, theology has in fact taken poverty seriously. The conclusion is that in order to understand the context, one must add the *quando* [when] to the *ubi* [where]. During those years something happened that changed theology. Reality, which occurs in time, has a *quando*, so one could say that this epoch was a *kairos* during which there was a discernment of the *signs of the times*. But I think something more radical occurred: the poverty that had always been there *irrupted*. It made itself noticed in a way that could not be hidden.

It is true that in the lives of believers and in theology, especially in its biblical roots, it has always been important to take reality into account. But reality can simply "be there," or it can "break in." The great events of the Bible are not simply "there" but rather "break in." In the Hebrew Scriptures the cries of slaves "broke in," and the God of the fathers "broke in" with his promise to always be with his people and bring them life. In the New Testament the sufferings of the poor, the sick and widows "broke in" (even though the language is not as strong as in the Exodus), and Jesus of Nazareth is described in the texts as having "broken in." He spoke with authority; no fear kept him from speaking the truth or constricted his liberty. He did not flee from conflicts, dangers, or death threats. His walking through Galilee was not a stroll, nor was his work reduced to doing good things; it involved conflict. Neither was he limited to communicating generic or only ethical truths, for his most central theme was prophecy. After going about doing good he died on a cross with "a loud cry" (Mk 15:38). His was not an agreeable death like that of Socrates or Seneca. In life and in death, Jesus "broke in." Indeed, the resurrection itself was not a prodigious event but rather an "irruption" of God.

This "irruption of reality" is what shapes theology. It is true that the mystery of God manifests itself in everyday life. But when reality "breaks in," the manifestation of God has a special quality. It shakes things up and forces us to think, to do theology.

The radical character of the irruption of reality cannot be required or programmed, and it does not offer reasons for its occurrence, even in intrinsically important circumstances. In my opinion while many things were well stated at Vatican II and, more recently, at Aparecida, I do not think that reality got to the point of "breaking in." It did break in at Medellín, in a way that the participants—and analogously the texts—did not simply amplify on Vatican II, but allowed themselves to be shaped by the reality that was powerfully "breaking in," which explains the impact it made.[22] Also the theology of liberation

---

22. In my view the 32nd General Congregation of the Society of Jesus, called by Pedro Arrupe, caused a fundamental irruption of reality when

has been built on this irruption. It was not built on and driven by an already constituted tradition or an already conceptualized doctrine, though some of the best theology Europe had to offer helped. The foundation and the beginning—what got theology going—was the irruption of the poor and of God in the poor, as was well understood at an early stage by Gustavo Gutiérrez.

We could say something similar about the christologies that were developing among us during this period. Without doubt the reflections from abroad by Karl Rahner, Jürgen Moltmann, Jacques Dupont, and Joachim Jeremias helped. But to bring about a rereading of the texts, it was essential for a reality to break in that reminded us of oppressed Galilee, and for human beings to break in who reminded us of Jesus: his compassion, his honesty about reality, his prophecy, his courage in the face of conflict, his fidelity undeterred even by the cross, his prayer, his trust in and availability to the Father-God. This is the Jesus who broke in as the Son, the one to whom we must conform ourselves, and the older brother we must follow. Both Son and brother became realities in Jesus.

The conclusion is clear. A theology grounded in the irruption of reality has, it is worth repeating, radical roots. Such a theology has problems by definition, since irruption does not occur every day, and it is not easy to maintain the light and the intensity that produced the original irruption. But whatever the difficulties in keeping them going, we have to overcome the temptation to ignore them. Pedro Casaldáliga, Jean Ziegler, and

---

it defined "the struggle for faith and the struggle for justice" as the crucial mission of our time ("Jesuits Today," Decree 2, of *Documents of the Thirty-Second General Congregation of the Society of Jesus*, [Washington, DC: Jesuit Conference, 1975] 12). I do not believe this irruption emerged as a conclusion of reflection, or even as a result of discernment. It came from outside, sovereignly, powerfully. The reality of injustice and idolatrous unbelief had irrupted along with the need to return to the essence of Christianity. From that point on 49 Jesuits have been assassinated in the Third World for struggling against injustice. I think this is proof that reality had irrupted and that reality was moving toward this crucial struggle.

Ignacio Ramonet tell us that realities continue to exist today capable of producing an equally or even more powerful impact than those that broke in to our context during the 1970s. Communication media, governments and political parties, and cultural, political and religious institutions, each in their own way, take charge of trivializing reality and of concealing it. And they try, above all, to keep it from becoming an irruption that generates praxis and theology.

Specifically with regard to theology, a variety of factors, but especially the costs, deter it from maintaining the original power of the inciting irruption: in society these factors include slander, persecution, and death; in the churches they take other forms. This has been evident in El Salvador. But it is also clear that if reality is not allowed to break in, the texts of the past become mute and do not give of themselves to the present.

The Epistemological Rupture

The irruption of reality in Latin America accompanied an *epistemological rupture* in theology. The most novel aspect of this movement was the act of relating theological reason and praxis (historical, ecclesial, and pastoral), on which theologians as diverse as Gustavo Gutiérrez and Hugo Assmann agreed. Here in El Salvador, inspired by Xavier Zubiri, Ellacuría elaborated and amplified a specific understanding of the meaning of intellective knowing. It should be applied to every form of intellective knowing, but in fact he more deeply analyzed the intellection of Latin American theology as a theology of liberation.[23]

Ellacuría's proposal turned out to be a novel one and, in important aspects, practically contrary to the epistemologies currently in use. For this reason I speak of an epistemological *rupture*, the foundation of which consists in the idea that intelligence should throw itself into reality. His proposal was that human intelligence must "apprehend reality and face up to it,"

---

23. Ellacuría, "Hacía una fundamentación filosófica del método teológico latinoamericano."

an assertion that he breaks into three dimensions: "grasping what is at stake in reality" (the *noetic* dimension) from Zubiri; to this Ellacuría added "assuming responsibility and paying the price for reality" (the *ethical* dimension), and "taking charge of reality" (the *praxis* dimension). For my part, more from experience and intuition than from theological reflection, I have added another step: "allowing oneself to be carried by reality" (the dimension of a *graced* intelligence).

Applying this proposal to *theological* intelligence, the notion of *taking charge of reality* led Ellacuría to define "theological intelligence" as "the ideological moment of ecclesial praxis,"[24] whose end was "the fullest realization possible in history of the kingdom of God."[25] For my part, I tried to pick up this intuition from Ellacuría and defined theology as *intellectus amoris* (*iustitiae, misericordiae*),[26] going a step beyond the *intellectus fidei* of Augustine and the *intellectus spei* of Moltmann in his *Theology of Hope*.

Emphasizing the praxis dimension of intelligence was not totally novel in Latin American theology, as I have said. I actually think the dimension of "assuming responsibility and paying the price for reality" was more novel and demanding. Ellacuría argues that intelligence "has not been given to humanity so that we might evade our real obligations, but rather so that we might pick up and carry on our shoulders what things really are, and what they really demand.[27] It is not possible to adequately grasp reality intellectively without the willingness to pick up what is burdensome in it—which is not usually taken seriously. The assassinated Ellacuría—thinker, philosopher, and theologian—can stand as a symbol for an intelligence that picked up reality.

---

24. Ellacuría, "La teología como momento ideológico de la praxis eclesial."

25. Ellacuría, "Aporte de la teología de la liberación a las religiones abrahámicas en la superación del individualismo y del positivismo," 9.

26. Sobrino, "Teología en un mundo sufriente."

27. Ellacuría, "Hacia una fudamentación," 419.

Nor is it by chance that Salvadoran theology has pioneered persecution and martyrdom as central themes for theology in a strict sense—not only pastoral or spiritual theology—because it picked up the reality that produced persecution and martyrdom.

There has also been a rupture in the way of "grasping what is at stake in reality," which implies "a being in the reality of things, and not merely a being before the idea of things, or a being in their meaning."

Thus understood, an exercise of the intelligence has as its referent the concrete reality that I have called the "context." And being adequately in the context, which is to say, "in the reality of things," the "texts" about Jesus were reread and intellectively known praxically, ethically, and gracefully. Let us see how.

"Taking charge of the reality [of Jesus]" (the *praxis* dimension) principally signified *constructing* the kingdom today, which made one better understand, through a certain affinity, what the kingdom proclaimed by Jesus meant: a kingdom of life, of justice, mercy, and hope. It also brings one to understand better all that Jesus did in service of the kingdom—his proclamation, mercy, prophecy. . . . It also certainly signified recognizing more clearly what constitutes the anti-kingdom, since dealing with reality in order to change it made one experience it as a negative, destructive, powerful, and opposing force. This in turn, *sub specie contrarii*, helped us Salvadoran theologians understand the kingdom. Further, through taking charge of the kingdom today, this improved understanding of both the kingdom and the anti-kingdom helped us "realize about" the person of Jesus, since the kingdom of God was not just one reality for him, or even the most important reality among others; rather it was that reality to which his life had a constitutive relationship.

"Assuming responsibility and paying the price for reality" (the ethical dimension) signified *picking up* what Jesus bore: persecution, slander, and torture by economic, military, cultural, religious powers. And again, through a certain affinity, that made it easier for us to "realize about" the cross of Jesus and its causes, as well as the crucified Jesus and his victimizers. "Assuming responsibility and paying the price for reality" helped us understand the crucified Jesus.

"Allowing oneself to be carried by reality" (the dimension of a graced intelligence) signified gracefully accepting a force and a light, as did those who "picked up Jesus." It is not easy—from the texts—to know what it was that historically "picked up Jesus" (another example is his experience of the Father). But at least this makes us ask if Jesus also experienced grace, and in what that might consist, a question not habitually asked in christology.

In a different context Rahner wrote some lucid words that help illuminate this dialectic of "carrying and being carried"—or in my terms: "picking up and being picked up." In one of his last writings he says that "being a Christian is a heavy-light burden, as the Gospel calls it. When we carry it, it carries us. The longer one lives, the heavier and the lighter it becomes."[28] Something similar, I think, has happened in El Salvador. We have had to pick up reality, but reality has also picked us up. Archbishop Romero had to pick up the repression of his people, but he said that "with this people it is not difficult to be a good pastor." In our context, then, in order to "realize about" Jesus, we must "pick him up." On the other hand, however, "Jesus picks us up."

The conclusion is that it is not enough "to be among concepts," if one wants to grasp intellectively who Jesus is. Instead, it is necessary today "to be among realities," analogous to how Jesus was among the realities of his day. Even a *kniende theologie* (kneeling theology) is not sufficient, as good and desirable as it might be. We must go through the epistemological rupture, throw ourselves into the real, take charge of it, pick it up, and allow ourselves to be carried by it. If we try to do it any other way, the texts give less of themselves.

Sometimes the texts have given of themselves the opposite of what we think was their original message. With no desire to

---

28. Rahner and Weger, *Our Christian Faith*, 178–79.

exaggerate, it is paradoxical, on the one hand, that the reality of Jesus of Galilee has been well investigated, and that these investigations have yielded important theoretical results. On the other hand, the reality thus attained has not had as powerful an effect on the reader and on the collective consciousness as it could and should have had, given that these concepts have not only "content" but also "weight."

Without *an irruption of reality* and *a rupture of the way of knowing intellectively*, the concept can be correct, but exceedingly trivial. In that case the reality behind the concept can remain far outside the grasp of theology and the collective consciousness, so that only with great difficulty can they unleash a living and creative thought process. But with the irruption of reality and an epistemological rupture, the concept has weight and can help transform the thinking subject, making demands and pushing the subject in that direction. It can become part of the collective consciousness and trigger an intense and creative process.

This is what I believe has occurred in the Third World with the concepts of *liberation* and the *historical Jesus*. They may of course be limited and always subject to improvement, but they have a special *pondus* [weight].[29] When one is truly in the midst of reality, and the intelligence takes charge of the cause of Jesus, picks it up, and allows oneself to be carried along by it, the concept can become not only precise and scientific but also powerful. It has a *pondus*. And this is usually transmitted, with limitations, of course, to the sayings of Jesus.

A final reflection on the context. I have spoken about its importance for making the text yield more and better of itself. But we must also remember what the New Testament scholar Xavier Alegre Santamaría frequently says: "a text outside its context

---

29. Christians and theologians have captured in "liberation" a concept of enormous depth and utility for putting hidden oppressions into words and for fomenting hopes of liberation [grounded in] the *pondus* of the concept itself. The credit for having presented the concept in this way must be given to Gustavo Gutiérrez, the pioneer of this work.

can be easily turned into a pretext." Although he is referring to the *context* in which the biblical *texts* were written, his warning can also be applied to the context in which those texts are read today. Without taking the context of present reality centrally into account, a text—as distinguished as the Gospel of John, for instance—can be reduced to shaping the personal experience of the believer (a very important thing), to information about the realities of the past, or as a reference to misty realities. And when this happens, the text becomes a pretext, an *excuse* for not having to face up to Jesus today, for not taking charge of what reality demands of us and makes possible in the present, and for not picking up its demands. . . .

—*The Galilean Jesus*, 439, 442–53; translated by Robert Lassalle-Klein
(with minor revisions from original translation)

"THOUGH THE MARTYRDOM OF THE JESUITS OBVIOUSLY CAUSED A SPECIAL PSYCHOLOGICAL IMPACT, IT HAS NOT BEEN THE ONLY DECISIVE MOMENT"

In October 1999 Hartono Budi, S.J., a young Jesuit, competed a dissertation on "The Christology of Jon Sobrino and Contemporary Martyrdom." I was the first reader and saw that Jon took Hartono's interest in the crucified people and his theology very seriously. About this time, Hartono made the thirty-day retreat completed by all Jesuits as part of "tertianship," the final stage of Jesuit formation, with Fr. Miguel Elizondo, S.J., former novice master of Central America (including Sobrino, Ellacuría, and most of the Central American Jesuit martyrs), and codirector of the famous Christmas 1969 retreat at which the Central American Jesuits embraced Medellín's "preferential option for the poor." These elements may explain why Jon responds in such depth to Hartono's questions about the impact of the University of Central America (UCA) murders on his christology, the role of reality as the core of his "method," the death of Archbishop

Romero, *what he calls the "Salvadoran school" of theology, what is most original in his thought, the core claims of the second volume of his christology, the impact of European theologians on his writings, and several other points. The letter represents a rare window into Sobrino's thoughts a decade after the November 1989 deaths of the UCA martyrs.*

San Salvador, June 30, 1999

To: Hartono Budi
        Berkeley, California
From: Jon Sobrino
        UCA, San Salvador

Dear Hartono.
I am sending you here some comments about your thesis. I have not been able to read it very thoroughly, but well enough, and, above all, the conclusions at the end of each chapter. In what follows I give you my general impressions, without going into detail about specific pages of your work. Perhaps these will help you to nuance certain points.

1. Overall, I think that you reflect my thinking well and highlight what might be more important and original. In that sense, the thesis is good. Obviously, the last chapter with criticisms is missing. Maybe it would be good from time to time to compare what I say with others, so that my theological thought would be clearer. But that would be a very long dissertation.

2. You mention "my method" several times. I understand that this is a major concern when writing a thesis. In my case, the fundamental method has been an intellectual journey driven by reality itself. In other words, it is not that I have decided to use a method of getting close to reality, but that reality has imposed itself on me. At least, that's what I think. In other words, before conceptualizing it, I think that, without seeking or attempting to do so, I found myself "grasping what is at stake in reality,"

"taking charge of reality," "assuming responsibility for reality," and "letting myself be carried by reality."[30]

In this, I found a teacher in Ellacuría, perhaps not so much on the last point. The most notable impact of reality [on my thought] has been "the crucifixion of peoples" and "the salvation brought by the crucified people." The latter is perhaps the most novel aspect of the theology that we have tried to do in El Salvador.

3. This impact of reality on my way of thinking has clearly been a process, running from the year 1974 until today. There have been "several" important moments in the process: 1970–1977 (the martyrdom of Rutilio Grande and the massacres of those years); 1977–1980 (the barbarous murders of priests and women religious culminating in Archbishop Romero and the brutal repression of the people); 1981–1989 (the group massacres of the Sumpul River and El Mozote, culminating with UCA murders).

In my real life, therefore, the [death of the] UCA martyrs has not been the only extraordinary moment, but rather have been others. My thought, consciously or unconsciously, has been affected by those events. But, though the martyrdom of the Jesuits obviously caused a special psychological impact, it has not been the only decisive moment. Maybe you can qualify this point in your thesis.

Another thing is the thinking published in my books, which represents a specific process. I believe that you do a good job of pointing it out in the analysis of my four books of christology. But the thought process has not been "mechanical," so to speak: before and after the murder of the Jesuits.

---

30. Editor's Note: I believe that Sobrino unintentionally inverts the order of the second and third moments of Ellacuría's triad here, which is not his usual practice (Sobrino places "hacerse cargo de la realidad" third, and "encargarse de la realidad" second).

4. Regarding the relationship with European theologians. Overall, you explain it well, but perhaps you should qualify it a little more. Moltmann's fundamental idea of the crucified God has been a constant in my christology, although nuanced and complemented by the idea of the crucified God[31] of Ignacio Ellacuría. I have not made much use of Pannenberg's theology, but rather have criticized it, though I have used his epistemology of the knowledge of God: to be able to make doxological assertions from historical ones. Regarding Rahner, I continue to appreciate above all his conception of the mystery of God and the sacramentalization of that mystery in the human. In the last two books I have used a lot of González Faus, with whom I share many of his ideas.

Again, this process of using European theologians and distancing myself from them on some important points has not been a mechanical one.

5. Regarding martyrs. I wrote about martyrdom for the first time in 1977 at the request of Archbishop Romero, and, undoubtedly, my conception of martyrdom has continued to develop over the years. Perhaps in this aspect, the most important martyrdom for my theology was that of Archbishop Romero. In any case, I think the most novel thing has been: 1) To conceive of martyrdom as a recapitulation of the life, praxis, and cross of Jesus, 2) And to also conceive of it as good news, due to the affinity is has with the crucified people. In my opinion, martyrdom, and even less martyrdom "like Jesus," has been little present in systematic theology.

6. In the second part of the book, "Faith in Jesus Christ," there are also reflections on the cross of Jesus when analyzing the different titles: high priest, messiah, and Son of God. I do not know

---

31. Given that the idea of "the crucified God" belongs to Moltmann, on whom Sobrino wrote his dissertation, one suspects that Sobrino means to say here, "the idea of the crucified people of Ignacio Ellacuría."

if you would be interested in integrating this into the thesis, albeit briefly.

7. In conclusion, I would like to recall what González Faus says in the review of "Faith in Jesus Christ" (in *Revista latinoamericana de teología* 46): my christology fundamentally says that Jesus Christ is good news, an *eu-aggelion*. I have this impression, and I think it is important to take note of it because, that, in my opinion, is the most original aspect of a christology of mercy, of the cross, and of martyrdom. In other words, cross and martyrs refer not only to "sin," but also to "grace." That seems to me the most important contribution of the "Salvadoran school" of theology (Ignacio Ellacuría, Archbishop Romero . . .) In the second part of "Faith in Jesus Christ" I emphasize the dimension of good news when analyzing the title of "Word" and in the final chapter of the second part: Jesus Christ as *eu-aggelion*.

As you can see, these are general observations that may help you to nuance some point or other, above all to not exaggeratedly make the martyrdom of the Jesuits the inflection point of my christology. As I said at the beginning, I think you have done very good work and I "recognize myself" in your writing. I thank you for the interest you have in doing theology from the crucified people. I hope it will help you when you return to your people.

Heartfelt greetings,
Jon

—"Letter to Hartono Budi"

4

Spirituality of Liberation:
Awakening from the Sleep
of Inhumanity

Sobrino's spirituality of liberation is grounded in gratitude and appreciation for the surprising encounter with God in the crucified people of El Salvador, tempered by a realistic awareness of their suffering caused by sin and idolatry. While "liberation and crucifixion provide the basic tension for Christian faith . . . on this continent,"[1] however, he insists that "the cross and martyrdom refer not only to 'sin,' but also to 'grace.'" He says, "This seems to me the most important contribution from the "Salvadoran school" of theology (Ignacio Ellacuría, Archbishop Romero . . .)."[2] And he adds, "I have allowed myself to be welcomed by God . . . , in a modest way . . . to be welcomed by the poor of this world, and to help the human family grow. Needless to say Jesus has opened my eyes to all of this."[3]

The section begins with Sobrino's exclamation that "in El Salvador I have been given the grace of meeting thousands of people like this Jesus of Nazareth." He describes the spirituality of the University of Central America (UCA) martyrs, who

---

1. Sobrino, *Jesus the Liberator*, 1.

2. Jon Sobrino, S.J., "Letter to Hartono Budi, S.J., June 30, 1999," personal files of Robert Lassalle-Klein, 2.

3. Gómez-Oliver and Benítez, *31 jesuítas se confiesan*, 494.

he believes "have opened a track in history along which it is easier to travel: . . . hunger and thirst for justice for the crucified people, . . . tireless analysis and condemnation of the truth about their crucifixion, and . . . steadiness and fidelity . . . in seeing them taken down from the cross." He recalls that in the UCA Jesuit community, "there was plain speaking about God's Kingdom and the option for the poor, sin and the following of Jesus." He explains, "We discovered that there are other sources of happiness" besides career, travel, and the usual fare. In answer to the question, "What is that?" he replies, "To not be ashamed of belonging to the human family! Being accepted . . . by normal people." And then, remarkably, he adds, "That a Jesuit might be assassinated the same way as a poor peasant in Aguilares. That's very important. . . . We can go to Aguilares now without feeling shame for being so different from them."

In trying to make sense of these claims, Sobrino says that "Ellacuría did what he did . . . because he was moved by reality," and that "Ellacuría's faith was carried by the faith of Archbishop Romero." But how exactly? Turning to Romero's conversion, Sobrino explains, "in his venture into the unknown and uncontrollable, in his moving forward without institutional church support, in his standing firm wherever the road might lead, you witnessed the Father who continues to be God." Sobrino's point, I believe, is that Ellacuría found in Archbishop Romero the path to an encounter with the reality of God, the God in the crucified people of El Salvador.

Building on what he calls, "this little obsession with reality," Sobrino then defines spirituality as "the spirit of a subject—an individual or a group—in its relationship with the whole of reality."[4] This presents the reader with a reconstructed understanding of what philosophers and theologians call "the hermeneutical circle."[5] For Sobrino, "the spirit of a subject" refers

---

4. Sobrino, *Spirituality of Liberation*, 13.

5. David Tracy says the hermeneutical circle of theology "articulates mutually critical correlations between . . . an interpretation of the Christian fact, and . . . an interpretation of the contemporary situation" (cf. Tracy, *Practical Theology*, 61–82.

to *"the subjective attitudes and virtues" that give "direction"
to, and "set in motion," the relationships, loves, commitments,
etc., of the human person toward the realities he or she encounters.*[6] *This reflects Ellacuría's corresponding notion that the historical reality of the subject is finally determined by his or her
response to the realities that are encountered. Lest the reader
miss the contrast between the jarring historical realism of this
approach and what Ellacuría calls the "reductionist idealism"
of many approaches to spirituality, Sobrino gives two examples
of what he believes spirituality is not. First, "spirituality is not
something . . . autonomous on the part of the subject; it stands in
relationship with reality"; and second, "this relationship is not
. . . a relationship with other spiritual realities only, but [rather]
a relationship with the totality of the real."*

*Sobrino then poses a series of questions, which he believes
that spirituality, particularly Latin American spirituality, must
face: "What is the correct relationship between the spirit of the
subject and the reality surrounding that subject?" What are "the
minimum demands of this relationship?" And what are "the prerequisites for spirituality as such, and thus for any and every
concrete spirituality?" He says, "We are looking for prerequisites that, once fulfilled, will become the foundations on which
spirituality will be built, if only the spirit of the subject remains
faithful to the internal dynamics of these presuppositions."*[7]

*Sobrino's answer is that "any genuine spirituality will demand
. . . (1) honesty about the real, (2) fidelity to the real, and (3) a certain correspondence by which we permit ourselves to be carried
along by the more of the real."*[8] *The Spanish text makes it immediately clear (which Sobrino does explicitly elsewhere) that these
are meant to echo Ellacuría's three famous dimensions of "confronting oneself with real things as real,"*[9] *and his corresponding*

---

6. Sobrino, *Jesus the Liberator*, 51.
7. Ibid., 14.
8. Sobrino, *Spirituality of Liberation*, 14.
9. Ellacuría, "Hacia una fundamentación del método teológico latino-americano," *ECA* 30, nos. 322–23, 419–20; and *Escritos teológicos*,
I, 207. See also Sobrino, "Jesus of Galilee from the Salvadoran Context:

notion that our apprehensions of reality place claims on us that cannot be ignored. He calls this our "bondedness" (or religación) to reality,[10] which means that when something is actualized as real for us, it creates a corresponding demand for self-actualization by the subject.[11] In other words, we are confronted with a whole series of decisions about whether and how to live by the truth of the realities we encounter. At the end of the day, therefore, our fundamental and unavoidable relationship with the "power of the real" presents us with a steady diet of choices regarding whether and how to appropriate our historical reality in relation to the realities we encounter.

Fair enough, but what is the reality about which Sobrino says we must be honest and faithful, and by which we may be "carried along"? Not surprisingly, he says that it is the historical reality of God's people, the majority of whom are struggling for life on the global margins of islands of wealth and privilege. And what should be the basic stance of followers of Jesus toward this reality? Sobrino says that common decency demands that we work to create a "civilization of poverty," in which everyone has enough to live and thrive, characterized by "mutual solidarity, in contrast to the closed and competitive individualism of the civilization of wealth." Speaking in 2014 to students at the Jesuit School of Theology of Santa Clara, he closed by saying, "My hope and desire is that all of you, graduates, professors, family members, Jesuits and others, work in such a way that the civilization of poverty not only remains a concept or ideal . . ., but indeed becomes a reality."[12]

Compassion, Hope, and Following the Light of the Cross," *Theological Studies* 70, no. 2: 449.

10. Zubiri, *El hombre y Dios,* 92–94, 139–40.

11. Ibid., 248.

12. "A Civilization to Humanize a Gravely Ill World," Graduation Speech, Jesuit School of Theology of Santa Clara, May 24, 2014.

"I HAVE BEEN GIVEN THE GRACE OF MEETING THOUSANDS OF PEOPLE LIKE JESUS OF NAZARETH"

In El Salvador I have been given the grace of meeting thousands of people like this Jesus of Nazareth. In March we recall Rutilio Grande and Monseñor Romero. In November we always remember the UCA Jesuits, with Julia Elba and Celina. In December we honor the four North American women, Ita, Maura, Dorothy, and Jean, as well as many hundreds of lay people and campesino men and women.　　　—"Foreword, with Gratitude and Hope," xiii.

"THE MARTYRS HAVE OPENED A TRACK IN HISTORY"

It is well known that the martyrdom of Ellacuría and his companions, because of its magnitude and international repercussions, and the historical moment when it occurred, undoubtedly helped bring about a negotiated end to the war. In addition to this, however, we must think about the salvation that Ellacuría and the martyrs leave us over time. This salvation is real. And it consists, I believe, in having generated an historical and real tradition, which is both supremely necessary and constructive. This means that by their life and death, these martyrs have opened a track in history along which it easier to travel: . . . hunger and thirst for justice for the crucified people, . . . tireless analysis and condemnation of the truth about their crucifixion, and . . . steadiness and fidelity . . . in seeing them taken down from the cross.

—"Ignacio Ellacuría, the Human Being and the Christian:
'Taking the Crucified People Down from the Cross,'"
in Burke and Lassalle-Klein, eds., *Love That Produces Hope*, 56

"THERE WAS PLAIN SPEAKING ABOUT GOD'S KINGDOM AND THE OPTION FOR THE POOR"

These men were also believers, Christians. I do not mention this here as something obvious or to be taken for granted, but as something central in their lives, something that really ruled all their lives. . . . When we spoke about matters of faith in the community, our words were sparing but really meant. We spoke about God's Kingdom and the God of the Kingdom, of Christian life as a following of Jesus, the historical Jesus, Jesus of Nazareth, because there is no other. In the university—in teaching and theological writings, of course—but also in solemn moments and public acts we recalled our Christian inspiration as something central, as what gave life, direction, force, and meaning to all our work, and explained the risks the university very consciously incurred. There was plain speaking about God's Kingdom and the option for the poor, sin and the following of Jesus. This Christian inspiration of the university was never just rhetoric when these Jesuits talked about it, and people understood that this was really the university's inspiration.

—"Companions of Jesus," 16

"IT WAS IMPORTANT TO DISCOVER THAT REALITY WAS FULL OF JOY"

For us Jesuits, when we first came in the 1950s, for my generation, including Ellacuría, the main difference was not being born in Central America . . . I don't think in those days we Spaniards made any efforts at inculturation. But the main problem in my opinion, was that both us Spaniards, but also the Central Americans, were distant from the reality of Central America. In other words, in simple, personal terms, when I came here . . . I saw very poor people walking barefooted in the street, and that shocked me. But it never occurred to me that I had to do something about it. To be a Jesuit, to be a priest in those days, coming from Spain, was to come to a country full of superstition. So, we were helping people to . . . become a little bit more like Spaniards, Europeans, or North Americans. That was the idea we had. Also, to help them to get married in the church. Things like that. So, I think that we not only lacked social conscience, but also the insight that faith in God had to do with looking at the poor and oppressed and asking ourselves what we had done, and what our responsibility was.

I was away most of the 1960s, and when I [initially] returned in 1972 I heard what had happened in the Province at the end of the sixties. What happened? Well, conversion! But what does that mean? I would say it meant discovering the reality that had always been there in front of us. We had it in front of our eyes, but we had not seen it. And what did that discovery mean? First of all, I would say in simple words . . . it made no sense to believe in God if we did not feel responsible towards other human beings. . . . Secondly, . . . to realize that we knew everything except for one thing: what it means to be a human being . . . We believed that to be a human being meant to be European. And that is still the case today in the United States or in Europe: that we are the real ones. . . . And then along with that, how can I say it, reality became both more dangerous for us, and for many other people of course. But it never occurred to me that reality could be dangerous; well, except, of course, in war and in . . . China, where atheism could . . . kill you. But that in Christian countries that reality could be risky, dangerous, never occurred to me or to us. Which, of course, was a way to introduce us to an awareness that society is permeated with sin.

And finally, it was important to discover that reality was full of joy. Joy. Not that the old sources of joy disappeared. For example, for us, having friends, or once in a while going to Spain, or getting a Ph.D., or publishing an article, or becoming famous. Those are the conventional sources of happiness. But besides that, we discovered that there are other sources of happiness. And what is that? To not be ashamed of belonging to the human family! Being accepted, accepted in general by the people, by normal people. That's a source of joy that is usually . . . not for us in general. . . . That a Jesuit might be assassinated the same way as a poor peasant in Aguilares. That's very important. . . . We can go to Aguilares now without feeling shame for being so different from them.

That, for me, is the main issue of what happened. And then the consequences are, well obvious, of trying to help others. Trying to be helped by others. Trying to make the suffering of others, our own sufferings. And also, that the joys of others might be our own joys. That is the change. And in that change, well, was a new way of communication to Ellacuría, who could conceptualize this in a very good way, that change had expressed itself in parishes, high schools and universities. Reality unfolded [revealed itself] for him, I'm convinced of that. And he realized that there is sin and that reality is dangerous, and risky, and also joyful. . . . The basic idea is that what is real, is real. That's the main discovery of people here in my perception. . . . All of a sudden you see things the way they are. Or, at least, you think you see things a little bit more the way they are than [you did] before. And that changes everything. Or at least that is the beginning of the process of change. . . .

And it's not just morals or ethics, but it's reality. And, how do you react in the midst of reality? I think that Ellacuría was pioneering that. Taking risks, not being, well, not afraid. We were, of course, but not being stopped by problems, persecution, bumps. That was very important for others to see that we were doing something real. And others might say, well, I don't want that. But that's, as I said, that's the key issue.

—Interview by Lassalle Klein, July 5, 1994, 2.

"ELLACURÍA DID WHAT HE DID BECAUSE HE WAS MOVED BY REALITY"

Ellacuría . . . had the gift to let reality talk.

— Interview by Lassalle-Klein, April 19, 1994, 1

Ellacuría did what he did not only because he had an idea, but because he was moved by reality. . . . If we go back, however, . . . and ask what helped him to conceptualize this reality, it was Zubiri and Rahner.

—Interview by Lassalle-Klein, March 17, 1994, 1

"I THINK ELLACURÍA'S FAITH WAS CARRIED BY THE FAITH OF ARCHBISHOP ROMERO"

I think that Archbishop Romero was a grace for Ellacuría in a very special way. I often thought that Ellacuría may have considered himself more or less a colleague of Zubiri in philosophy and colleague of Rahner in theology. . . . But he never considered himself a colleague of Archbishop Romero. And the reason is because he always saw Archbishop as someone who was ahead of him, as in the way Archbishop Romero placed himself before the mystery of the ultimate, [his] faith in God. As I have written, . . . I think his [Ellacuría's] faith was carried . . . by the faith of Archbishop Romero. In other words, he found in Archbishop someone who had the power, without imposing, "to draw you" toward him in faith. That is the grace.

—"El padre Ellacuría sobre Monseñor Romero," 136–37;
translated by Robert Lassalle-Klein

"IN ARCHBISHOP ROMERO YOU SAW THAT HOPE IS MORE REAL THAN ABSURDITY"

In Archbishop Romero, in his compassion for the suffering, his denunciations in their defense, his uncompromising love, you witnessed the God who is "Father" of the poor. In his conversion, his venture into the unknown and uncontrollable, in his moving forward without institutional church support, in his standing firm wherever the road might lead, you witnessed the Father who continues to be "God." And perhaps in Archbishop Romero, you also saw that, in spite of everything, commitment is more real than nihilism, joy is more real than sadness, and hope is more real than absurdity.

—"El padre Ellacuría sobre Monseñor Romero," 126;
translated by Robert Lassalle-Klein

FOUNDATIONS OF SPIRITUALITY:
REALITY AS MEDIATION FOR OUR
RELATIONSHIP WITH GOD

In this chapter I propose simply to sketch the structure of a spirituality of liberation, leaving an examination of the more concrete content of that spirituality for another time.

I must begin with the fact that there is such a thing as a Christian practice of liberation, and that therefore there must be a spirituality underlying this practice. True, the theology of liberation has dealt more explicitly with the practice of liberation than with its spirituality. Implicitly, however, a great deal has already been said. When we speak of following Jesus, of listening to God's word and putting it into practice, of embracing the situation, the cause, and the lot of the poor, we have already made important assertions about the Christian spirituality that "informs" the practice of liberation. But we may not yet have explicitated the structure of spirituality as such.

Let me turn to that task, then, and let me begin by stating what spirituality is. Spirituality is simply the spirit of a subject—an individual or a group—in its relationship with the whole of reality. This proposition . . . contains two important bits of information. First, it reminds us that spirituality is not something absolutely autonomous on the part of the subject; it stands in relationship with reality. Secondly, my descriptive definition implies that this relationship with reality is not a "regional" (restricted) relationship, or a relationship with other spiritual realities only, but a relationship with the totality of the real.

I think it important to underscore the "relational" character of spirit vis-á-vis the sum total of reality. First, this is an underlying intuition of the practice of liberation, and so it will have to underlie its spirituality, as well. Secondly, we must take care to avoid the temptation (frequent enough when it comes to the framing of a spirituality, as history shows) to "leave reality to itself"—to avoid the historical. To succumb to this temptation is to welcome into our lives an alienating parallelism in which the spiritual life and historical activity never meet. Here we shall be caught either in a subtle accommodation to whatever history will happen to offer "on its own"—and history will leave us behind—or in a no less subtle flight to a simple anticipation of the eschatological—leaving history behind.

Lest we fall victim to these temptations, and fail to make any progress in our understanding of spirituality, let us ask ourselves: What is the correct relationship between the spirit of the subject and the reality surrounding that subject? What would constitute the minimum demands of this relationship? What would be the prerequisites for spirituality as such, and thus for any and every concrete spirituality? We are looking for prerequisites that, once fulfilled, will become the foundations on which a spirituality will be built, if only the spirit of the subject remains faithful to the internal dynamics of these presuppositions.

There are three such prerequisites, it seems to me. Any genuine spirituality will demand, in the concrete: (1) honesty about the real, (2) fidelity to the real, and (3) a certain "correspondence" by which we permit ourselves to be carried along by the "more" of the real. These three basic attitudes can be converted into mediations of our relationship with God, so that these presuppositions and foundations are also objectively theological.[13]

In Latin America, we have rediscovered these presuppositions, or at least we have clarified them for ourselves, in the practice of liberation. And this rediscovery has facilitated their rediscovery by us in the life, practice, and destiny of Jesus.

—*Spirituality of Liberation*, 13–14

---

13. The original Spanish says, "por lo cual los presupuestos y fundamentos son también teologales," which should be translated, "so that these presuppositions and foundations are also theologal." *Theologal* means "related to God," as opposed to *theological,* which refers to the study of theology.

"BY *SPIRIT*, I MEAN . . ."

"In the Spirit" vs. "With Spirit"

"In my opinion, rather than talking about the spirit, theology should speak *in the Spirit* and *with spirit*."

—"A Su Aire," 496 [emphasis added]

"Spirit of the Subject"

By the spirituality of persecution and martyrdom I mean the spirit with which they must be confronted. . . . Before addressing this theme, let me make a few brief preliminary observations.

1) I propose to focus my attention in this chapter on the *spirit of the individual or group subject.* That is, I propose to examine the subjective attitudes and virtues that will enable a person or persons to face persecution and martyrdom courageously and with full awareness, and to render them both fruitful in terms of Christian values. I shall not, therefore, be analyzing the objective reality of persecution and martyrdom, although I shall have occasion to refer to it.

2) By "spirit" I mean, of course, the Christian spirit, which will already be familiar in its general lines to subjects of spirituality before their encounter with persecution and martyrdom, but which will achieve its plenitude as Christian precisely in that encounter. The Christian spirit becomes known in the measure in which it becomes reality.

3) Although spirit is a reality of a *subject*, it has a relationship with the objective reality of persecution and martyrdom. Thus spirituality is never totally autonomous or intentional, either in its content or with respect to the degree of its intensity. Rather it develops in strict relationship with its real object [e.g., persecution and martyrdom].

—*Spirituality of Liberation*, 88–89 [emphasis added]

"Spirit of God" vs. "Following with Spirit" by the Human Subject

Today, with the proliferation of movements relying on the Spirit (more as an expression of the marvelous and esoteric than as the reality that inspires following of Jesus), in which—with all due respect—the Spirit sometimes seems to be invoked as a *deus ex machina* rather than as the Spirit of the God of Jesus Christ, it is incumbent on us to stick to the thesis: the Spirit gives us strength to follow, but the following—and not esoteric conceptions—is the proper setting for the Spirit. The way that leads to knowledge of Jesus Christ is "following with spirit" but not the action of the Spirit cut off from following.

This is my basic thesis, and I should like to illustrate it now from the life of Jesus of Nazareth. Once the basic structure of this life has been established, we need to examine whether and how the Spirit becomes present in it, so that following Jesus will—for us—be carrying out in history not just a life "deprived of spirit" but one "full of spirit." In other words, the Spirit is made present not only in *the subjectivity* of those who follow Jesus but also in the *object* of their following. If we go back to Jesus' life, then, we find, on the one hand, that he said little about the Spirit and nothing about its personality, but, on the other, that he is described by the evangelists as possessed by the Spirit of God: at his baptism, in the temptations, at the start of his public life in the synagogue at Nazareth, and so on. The synoptic tradition even reifies this Spirit to some degree by regarding it as a "power" *(exousia, dynamis)*: "power had gone forth from him" (Mk 5:30; Lk 8:46).

More than this reifying (and personalizing) interpretation of this power that went forth from Jesus, however, the synoptics show what I see as more primary and basic: Jesus' life is shot through with a special power; it is a life "inspired by the Spirit of God," which means that following Jesus at this point of history will be following someone who, in his lifetime, was filled with the Spirit, and so following this "Jesus with spirit" will include his followers' readiness to let themselves be affected by whatever "spirit" might be for them. (Although the distinction is not always clear, I am using "Spirit" and "Spirit of God" [capital S] to refer to the Holy Spirit, the third person of the Trinity, and "spirit" [lower case] to refer to the Spirit's actual manifestations in history.)

The fact that Jesus lived, worked, and died "with spirit" is undeniable. There is no way his life can be seen as something mechanical: he is shown as coming up against the real world of his time in a particular, novel, and unflagging manner. These particular "ways" of coming up against the real world are the "spirit" with which he lived in the various spheres of life, which can—later, from faith—be interpreted as manifestations of the Spirit of God. Let us now look, systematically, at these manifestations of the Spirit in Jesus: the Spirit of *newness,* the Spirit of *truth and life*, the Spirit of *ecstasy* toward the Father.

— *Christ the Liberator*, 328–29

"I BEGAN TO AWAKEN FROM THE SLEEP OF INHUMANITY"

I have been asked to write about "how my mind has changed," and I must say that it has changed indeed—though not just my mind, I hope, but my will and heart as well. Because the changes that I have experienced and will write about have also been experienced by many others in El Salvador and throughout Latin America, I will be using singular and plural pronouns interchangeably.

I am writing for the North American reader, who, almost by definition, has difficulty understanding the Latin American reality and the deep changes which that reality can bring about. I will therefore try to explain the essence of such fundamental change from the perspective of El Salvador, comparing it with another change which is often said to lie at the heart of so-called modern Western civilization. From the time of Kant, such change has been described as an awakening from a "dogmatic slumber"— an awakening that is like the liberation of reason from subjection to authority and which, in turn, gives rise to the dogmatic proclamation that the fundamental liberation of the human being lies in the liberation of reason.

In the Third World, the fundamental change also consists of an awakening, but from another type of sleep, or better, from a nightmare—the sleep of inhumanity. It is the awakening to the reality of an oppressed and subjugated world, a world whose liberation is the basic task of every human being, so that in this way human beings may finally come to be human.

Such is the change that has occurred in me and in many others. And what has brought about such a profound and unexpected change is encounter with the reality of the poor and the victims of this world. In order to put all this in simple terms, permit me to offer a bit of biographical background prior to more deliberate reflection.

I was born in 1938 in Spain's Basque region, where I grew up. In 1957, I came to El Salvador as a novice in the Society of Jesus, and since then I have lived in this country, with two notable interruptions: five years in St. Louis studying philosophy and engineering, and seven years in Frankfurt studying theology. So I know fairly well both the world of development and abundance and the world of poverty and death.

I must confess that until 1974, when I returned to El Salvador, the world of the poor—that is, the real world—did not exist for me. When I arrived in El Salvador in 1957, I witnessed appalling poverty, but even though I saw it with my eyes, I did not really see it; thus that poverty had nothing to say to me for my own life as a young Jesuit and as a human being. It did not even cross my mind that I might learn something from the poor. Everything which was important for my life as a Jesuit I brought with me from Europe —and if anything had to change, that would come from Europe as well. My vision of my task as a priest was a traditional one: I would help the Salvadorans replace their popular "superstitious" religiosity with a more sophisticated kind, and I would help the Latin American branches of the church (the European church) to grow. I was the typical "missionary," full of good will and Eurocentricity—and blind to reality.

Further studies in philosophy and theology induced a rude awakening from "dogmatic slumber." During those years of study, my fellow students and I went through Kant and Hegel, through Marx and Sartre, and engaged in serious questioning at every stage. To put it bluntly, we began questioning the God we had inherited from our pious Central American, Spanish, and Basque families. We delved into exegetical criticism and Bultmann's demythologizing, into the legacy of modernism and the relativism of the church—all of which took one logically to a profound questioning not only of what we had been taught by the church, but also of the Christ.

We had to awaken from the dream. Awakening was painful and wrenching in my case; it was as if layers of skin were being removed one by one. Fortunately, there was light as well as darkness in the awakening. Karl Rahner's theology—I mention him because he was for me the one who left the most lasting and beneficial impression—was my companion during those years, and his pages on the mystery of God continue to accompany me even today. Vatican II gave us new insights and new enthusiasm; it helped us realize that the church is not itself the most important thing, not even for God. In working on my doctoral thesis on Christology, I began again to discover Jesus of Nazareth. He was not the abstract Christ I had imagined before, nor was he the Christ being presented by Pierre Teilhard de Chardin as "the final point of all evolution," nor by Rahner as "the absolute bearer of all salvation." I discovered that the Christ is none other than Jesus and that he conceived a utopia on which all too few have focused: the ideal of the kingdom of God.

The churchly triumphalism of our youth was far behind us now. We considered ourselves avant-garde and "progressive," even thinking ourselves well prepared to set the Salvadoran people on the right track. Nevertheless, even with many changes for the better, we had not changed fundamentally. I, at least, continued to be a First World product, and if I *was* changing, it was in accordance with that First World's process, at that world's pace, and by that world's laws. Although it was a necessary change in many ways, it was insufficiently radical and, from a Third World point of view, it was superficial. For me, the world continued to be the First World, the church continued to be the European church of Vatican II, theology continued to be German theology, and utopia continued to mean that in some way the countries of the south would become like those of the north. That was what many of us wanted, consciously or not, to work for at that time. We had awakened from the dogmatic slumber, if you will, but we continued to sleep in the much deeper sleep of inhumanity—the sleep of egocentrism and selfishness. But eventually we did wake up.

Through one of those strange miracles which happen in history, I came to realize that while I had acquired much knowledge and gotten rid of much traditional baggage, deep down nothing had changed. I saw that my life and studies had not given me new eyes to see this world as it really is, and that they hadn't taken from me the heart of stone I had for the suffering of this world.

That realization is what I experienced upon returning to El Salvador in 1974. And I began, I believe, to awaken from the sleep of inhumanity. To my surprise, I found that some of my fellow Jesuits had already begun to speak of the poor and of injustice and of liberation. I also found that some Jesuits, priests, religious, farmers, and students, even some bishops, were acting on behalf of the poor and getting into serious difficulties as a consequence. Having just arrived, I didn't know what possible contribution I might make. But from the beginning it became quite clear that truth, love, faith, the gospel of Jesus, God, the very best we have as people of faith and as human beings—these were somehow to be found among the poor and in the cause of justice. I do not mean to imply that Rahner and Jürgen Moltmann, whom I studied avidly, no longer had anything to say to me. But I did come to understand that it was absurd to go about trying to Rahnerize or Moltmannize the people of El Salvador. If there was something positive I could bring from the perspective of my studies, the task would have to be the reverse: If at all possible, we needed to Salvadorize Rahner and Moltmann.

At this point, I was fortunate enough to find others who had already awakened from the sleep of inhumanity, among them Ignacio Ellacuría and Archbishop Oscar Romero, to name just two great Salvadoran Christians, martyrs, and friends. But beyond those happy encounters, little by little I came face-to-face with the truly poor, and I am convinced that they were the ones who brought about the final awakening. Once awakened, my questions—and especially my answers to questions—became radically different. The basic question came to be: Are we really human and, if we are believers, is our faith human? The reply was not the anguish which follows an awakening from dogmatic sleep, but the joy which comes when we are willing not only to change the mind from enslavement to liberation, but also to change our vision in order to see what had been there, unnoticed, all along, and to change hearts of stone into hearts of flesh—in other words, to let ourselves be moved to compassion and mercy.

The jigsaw puzzle of human life, whose pattern had broken apart as we went through a period of analysis and questioning, again broke apart when we met the poor of this world. But there was a significant difference. Following the awakening from dogmatic sleep, we had the hard task of piecing the puzzle together again, and we obtained some rather positive results. But such a first awakening was not enough to shake us from ourselves. Wakening from the sleep of inhumanity was a stronger jolt, but a more joyous one. It is possible to live an intellectually honest life in this world, but it is also possible to live sensitively and joyfully. And then I realized another long-forgotten fact: The gospel is not just truth—which must be reconciled in the light of all our questioning—but is, above all, good news which produces joy.

In reflecting on this questioning and this joyful change, I would like to zero in on what is most important: the new eyes we receive when we awaken from the sleep of inhumanity to the reality of what is fundamental. . . .

In El Salvador, we have awakened to the fact that a heartless humanity manages to praise works of mercy but refuses to be guided by the mercy principle. Guided by this principle, we have discovered some important things.

First of all, we well know that in our world there are not just wounded individuals but crucified peoples, and that we should enflesh mercy accordingly. To react with mercy, then, means to do everything we possibly can to bring them down from the cross. This means working for justice—which is the name love acquires when it comes to entire majorities of people unjustly oppressed—and employing in behalf of justice all our intellectual, religious, scientific, and technological energies.

Second, we must realize that mercy that becomes justice will automatically be persecuted by the powerful, and therefore mercy must be clung to vigorously and consistently. The Salvadoran martyrs—alternately called subversives, communists, and atheists—were consistently merciful. That is why they struggled for justice, and that is why they were assassinated.

Third, we must give mercy priority above all else. This is no easy task for any civil institution, any government, business, political movement, or army, nor for any religious or ecclesial institution. One must be willing to risk for mercy, the way Archbishop Romero did, risking not only one's personal life but even the ecclesial institution itself. That is why he had to witness the destruction of his archdiocese's radio and printing operations and why some of the priests around him were assassinated. All must be risked, because what is first of all is the ultimate.

Fourth, I have learned that the exercise of mercy is the measure of freedom—that state of being universally hailed as a human ideal in the Western world. When he healed on a Sabbath, Jesus was violating the rules and norms of his time because he was merciful, not because he was a liberal. Jesus understood freedom from the point of view of mercy, not the other way around. For him, freedom meant that nothing could stand in the way of the exercise of mercy.

This mercy is the demand which has been placed in our hearts by the Salvadoran reality. But the demand is also a blessing, is also good news. "Happy are the merciful," Jesus says. From this point, we can reinterpret the other Beatitudes. "Happy are those who hunger and thirst for justice. Happy are those who work for peace. Happy are you when you are persecuted for the cause of justice." And if we use the Beatitudes to reinterpret what we said above about acquiring new eyes, we can also say, "Happy are those with a clean heart." Finally, if mercy and new vision are placed at the service of the poor and we thus participate to some degree in their lot, we too can hear, "Happy are the poor." . . .

To sum up, then: We have awakened from a sleep of inhumanity to a reality of humanity. We have learned to see God from the point of view of the victimized, and we have tried to see this world of the victimized from the point of view of God. We have learned to exercise mercy and find joy and a purpose for life in doing so.

Remembering my dear Jesuit brother Ignacio Ellacuría, rector of Jose Simeon Cañas Central American University, who was murdered with five other Jesuits and two pious women on November 16, 1989, I have learned that there is nothing as vital in order to live as a human being than to exercise mercy on behalf of a crucified people, and that nothing is more humanizing than to believe in the God of Jesus. As I have seen this way of life become very real in many Salvadorans, in many other Latin Americans, and in many who sympathize with us in various places, another new thing I have learned . . . is the importance of saying "Thank you." Then life and faith still make sense.

— *The Principle of Mercy*, 1–4, 10–11;
translated by Dimas Planas

TWENTY-FIVE YEARS AFTER THE ASSASSINATIONS: HUMANIZING A GRAVELY ILL WORLD

Dear Friends,
I want to start by thanking the faculty, administration and board of the Jesuit School of Theology of Santa Clara University for their invitation to address the students who are graduating

today, as well as the professors and family members who have accompanied them during their studies.

My presence here today brings back memories that I greatly appreciate. Twenty-five years ago JST conferred to me an *honorary doctorate*. This was a way of honoring my Jesuit brothers and two simple women who had been betrayed and assassinated in the middle of the night just a few weeks before.

Years have passed; however, I still find inspiration in those men and women to address you. The six Jesuits, like many of us who are gathered here, worked in a university. Amando Lopez, Juan Ramón Moreno and Ignacio Ellacuría were theologians—the latter is well-known internationally and especially at JST. Segundo Montes was a *sociologist* who accompanied migrants in Honduras and took up their cause before the United States Congress. Ignacio Martín-Baró was a *social psychologist* who analyzed the violence perpetrated against the common people. Joaquín López y Lopez, was *co-founder* of UCA and *founder* of *Fe y Alegría*. The two women, Elba and Celina, mother and daughter, were *workers* like the people here who are in charge of maintenance, cleaning, gardening, and cooking. They were a symbol of the men and women whom Monseñor Romero loved to the end, a crucified people, a people poor and hopeful. Remembering them all, and drawing on the thinking of Ignacio Ellacuría, I will offer some reflections on what, in my opinion, is the greatest problem facing our world today, a world into which we send our graduates. I also will touch on what we have to do.

A World Gravely Ill. The Civilization of Wealth

The most real, most hurtful, and most puzzling truth is that our world is in bad shape. During his final days in 1989, devoid of all youthful exaltations, Ignacio Ellacuría said tersely that "our civilization is gravely ill."[14] In 2005, Jean Ziegler, Special

---

14. Ignacio Ellacuría, "El desafío de las mayorías pobres," 1078.

Representative to the United Nations regarding the right to food, said that the world was "threatened to death by massive financial capital." A few days ago, the Venezuelan theologian, Pedro Trigo, wrote that the current reality of forced migrations—of which you have experience here in California—expresses, "in all its harshness, magnitude, and hard-heartedness, the sin of the world."[15]

Myopic, misleading, or hypocritically-maintained tributes to globalization cannot hide the disease that threatens our world, and Ellacuría warned of the dangers of "a fateful and fatal outcome." Denouncing these false tributes, he maintains that this sickness is produced by the *civilization of wealth*. And he concluded that in order to avoid the danger, we have to "reverse, subvert, and launch history in another direction." Some hopeful progressives say that today "another world is *possible*." Ellacuría argued that "another world is *necessary*." And for that *other* world to burst into reality, another civilization is needed, a civilization that opposes and overcomes the present civilization. He named it *the civilization of poverty*.[16] . . .

In the civilization of wealth, the *motor* that drives history is "the private accumulation of the greatest possible capital on the part of individuals, groups, multinationals, states, or groups of states." Its meaning is the maximum *enjoyment* of that accumulation based on its own security and the possibility of an ever-growing consumerism as the basis for happiness itself.

This civilization is not located geographically because it is present "in the East as well as in the West and deservedly is called capitalist civilization (whether state capitalism or private

---

15. Pedro Trigo, "Horizonte cristiano de la pastoral de la movilidad," *RLT* 91 (2014) 3, and note 1.

16. Ignacio Ellacuría, "Utopía y profetismo desde América Latina," *ECA* 17 (1989): 170, 173; trans, "Utopia and Prophecy in Latin America." *Mysterium Liberationis: Fundamental Concepts of Liberation Theology*, (Maryknoll, NY: Orbis Books, 1993), 289–328.

capitalism)." The judgment that we make about it should not be simplistic, for that civilization "has brought benefits to humanity that, as such, should be preserved and furthered (scientific and technical development, new modes of collective consciousness, and so forth). But it has also brought *greater evils.*" For instance: 1) it does not satisfy the basic needs of all; 2) it not only does *not* generate equality but it is not capable of doing so; and 3) it does not generate a humanizing spirit.

The *first point* is a crime. It is the denial of life. It causes the slow death that results from poverty or hunger, and the violent death that comes to those who rebel and struggle for life.

People who wield great power often hide the *second point,* but they are not convincing. There are simply not enough resources on this planet for the level of enjoyment of what has been accumulated to be universally enjoyed. Following the insight of the philosopher Immanuel Kant, the civilization of wealth is unethical precisely because it is not universalizable. Whatever the song sung by the sirens—whether they say that evil is not as absolutely bad as it may seem, or that the good follows its path, or that reprogramming efforts will reduce poverty by 2025, etc.—what remains undeniable is the fact that the level of life (and not just the level of life of the millionaires, but even the level of life of middle-class Americans, Europeans or Japanese) is not universalizable. They consume so many resources, raw materials and energy, that what remains is simply not enough for the rest of the world's population to live well.

This makes it difficult or impossible for the human spirit to flourish as a dimension of the totality of a civilization, the *third* of these evils. It is the negation of mutual support and universal dignity—whatever the formulations on the Universal Declaration of Human Rights might be. Ellacuría insisted with increasing force that the civilization of wealth does not generate the spirit, inspiration, energy or values capable of humanizing people and societies. The civilization of wealth is the civilization of the individual, of a selfish "good life," and of a type of success that excludes others and comes at their expense. . . .

As stated, the civilization of wealth is not defined geographically, although it is more established in some regions than others. Although said respectfully and with recognition, for Ellacuría, the United States is a paradigm of such a civilization, and those countries configured along these lines act as if they themselves are endowed with a type of Manifest Destiny.

Such a spirit dehumanizes. It tends to generate contempt in some people and servile or irrational, violent responses in others. In 1989, without referring to its economic means, but rather to its spiritual potential, Ellacuría said that the United States "has a bad solution"[17] and added that a bad solution is worse than having no solution, as is in the case in the Third World. Generalizing, he concluded that countries of abundance have "no hope"—while hope is very much a reality in the Third World. On the contrary, he said, what characterizes these countries of abundance, spiritually, is fear.

Looking at the world in its entirety, that is, at the world of Ellacuría and at our world today, one cannot see how such a world has meaning, especially when we consider that the parable of the rich man and poor Lazarus remains *the* dominant parable, the one which describes the situation in its entirety. Ellacuría's conclusion is lapidary: the civilization of wealth is a "humanistic and moral disaster."[18] And passing judgment on its long history, he added that the self-correcting processes of such a civilization are not sufficient to reverse its destructive course.

A World on the Way to Healing: "The Civilization of Poverty"

What can heal this world is what Ellacuría calls "a *civilization of poverty*." I hope I can explain it well so that it remains for you graduates in theology an enduring legacy.

---

17. "Quinto Centenario . . .", 277, 282.
18. "Utopía y profetismo desde América Latina," 173.

Already in the first article in which he addressed this theme, Ellacuría programmatically defined the civilization of poverty as "a universal state of affairs that guarantees the satisfaction of basic needs, the freedom to make personal choices, and a space for personal and communal creativity that shapes new forms of life and culture; these in turn engender new relationships with nature, with other human beings, within oneself, and with God."[19]

This could be considered the most general expression of utopia. It is *specific* to the civilization of poverty when the foundations of such a civilization are discussed. It is "founded on a materialist humanism transformed by Christian light and inspiration."[20] In the first place, this expression touches on the ability to humanly engage material reality. And thus, as also articulated by Pope John Paul II in his encyclical *Laborem Exercens,* what is being put forth here is a civilization based on *work,* that is, not only that which *produces,* but also that which *channels creativity* and human fulfillment, a civilization that humanizes more than a civilization which produces only economic capital.

In the second place, this civilization of poverty is permeated by important elements of the Jesus-centered Biblical tradition. And in the case of Ellacuría, the Ignatian contemplation of the Two Standards likewise is functioning and is being appropriately historicized, materially and socially.[21] I wish to elaborate on this point a bit since this school is rooted in Ignatian spirituality. In his *Spiritual Exercises,* Ignatius presents two paths, one which leads to salvation and the other to condemnation. One starts with poverty and means that the person following this path, like Christ, will also experience insults and humiliations. We recognize this path as one of humility, one which leads to authentic good. The other path, on the contrary, begins with wealth and is furthered by worldly and vain honors, overweening pride, and

---

19. "El Reino de Dios y el paro en el tercer mundo," 595.
20. "Utopía y profetismo desde América Latina," 170.
21. "Lectura latinoamericana de los Ejercicios Espirituales de San Ignacio," 128–33.

an integral dehumanization that leads to evil. Both standards, by their very nature, are in opposition to each other.

Within this Ignatian understanding, poverty is the key and Ellacuría insists on the need to work for a civilization of poverty. Therefore, it is not enough to prophetically preach this civilization against the civilization of wealth. It is not even enough to simply proclaim it as good news for the poor of this world. Ellacuría says that the solution "cannot be in escaping from this world and confronting it with a sign of prophetic protest, but in entering into it to renew it and transform it in the direction of the utopia of the new earth."[22] Because it is dialectical and contrary to the prevailing civilization, one cannot work for the civilization of poverty without suffering persecution and defamation. That would be a vain illusion. The multitude of martyrs for justice in Latin America since Medellín is clear proof of this fact.

Within the context of building this civilization of poverty, Ellacuría proposes two fundamental tasks. The first, more understandable and acceptable in principle, is to "create economic, political and cultural models that enable a civilization of work as a substitute for a civilization of capital." The other task is to strengthen "mutual solidarity, in contrast to the closed and competitive individualism of the civilization of wealth."

With solidarity we enter a sphere of reality that not only has to do with instrumental efficacy. It is the sphere of the "Spirit," that which is truly spiritual. In his final years, Ellacuría insisted that it is the Spirit which must inform this new civilization, and it must be generated principally by the poor. It seems to me that this is the most striking aspect of Ellacuría's thought during his final years, when he analyzed the global social reality: his insistence that the new civilization be informed by Spirit, a spirit generated mainly by the poor. The poor in their plentitude are

---

22. "Utopía y profetismo desde América Latina," 172.

the poor with spirit, and the civilization which they humanize is a civilization of Spirit.

In a second article that Ellacuría developed within an explicitly Christian context, he wrote:

> This poverty authentically gives space to the Spirit. People will no longer be stifled by the desire to have more than others, by lustful desires to have all sorts of superfluities when most of humanity lacks basic necessities. Then, the spirit will be able to flourish, that immense spiritual and human wealth of the poor and of the people of the Third World, who are now choked by poverty and by the imposition of 22 cultural models more suitable for other settings, but not necessarily more humane.[23]

In conclusion, if you will permit me a bit of irony, I like to say that "in the liturgy, things always go well for God." My sincere desire is that things will go well for God in the civilization of the poor. In other words, I hope that this divine vision becomes historical reality.

My hope and desire is that all of you, graduates, professors, family members, Jesuits and others, work in such a way that the civilization of poverty not only remains a concept or ideal within our liturgy, but indeed becomes a reality.

In this civilization of poverty, may the poor be our sisters and brothers. They are the very ones who inspired the martyrs I mentioned in the beginning of this talk. These poor persons also loved and inspired four North American women, Maura, Ita, Dorothy, and Jean who also gave their lives for this civilization.

Let me close with the same words with which Ellacuría ended his final theological essay. He speaks here about the "new human beings" who emerge with the civilization of poverty:

---

23. Ibid., 184.

These new human beings, for their part, keep on announcing, firmly and steadfastly although always in darkness, a future that is ever greater, because beyond all these futures, as they follow one upon another, they catch sight of the God who saves, the God who liberates.[24]

May you, the graduates of today, become these new human beings!

Thank you.

—"A Civilization to Humanize a Gravely Ill World,"

---

24. Ibid.

Conclusion

"With Dean Brackley, God Visited Us"

This article was published on October 27, 2011, the last day of the nine-day vigil for Dean Brackley. Jon invited me into his office and excitedly showed me the edition of "Letter to the Churches," which Christians for Peace in El Salvador (CRISPAZ), used to publish for him in Texas when it was too dangerous to publish it in El Salvador. He leaned over the desk, and said, "Take a look. I stayed up all night. I never do that! But I really wanted to finish this for Dean's funeral. What do you think?" I quickly paged through the issue and came upon a version of his, "Letter to Ellacuría," where readers are able to catch an annual glimpse into Jon's heart and mind. As I read through the letter, I was stunned to find that Ellacuría's famous phrase, "With Archbishop Romero, God visited El Salvador," had been altered to read, "with Dean Brackley, God visited us." Was Jon really including Dean in the holy trinity of Rutilio Grande, Archbishop Romero, and Ignacio Ellacuría? He then told me that Dean had refused the offer to intern his body with those of the martyrs in the University of Central America (UCA) chapel and had insisted that he be buried with the regular Jesuits in the province cemetery. Stunning: Not that Dean would refuse the honor, but that it would be offered. Dean was the only one of the ten Jesuits who were missioned to El Salvador after the assassinations who had been able to stay. Suffice to say, many considered it a miracle of generosity and grace that any outsider, but

especially one from the country that had trained the assassins,[1]
could so humbly and joyfully fit in. It is my view that, in using
this revered phrase for Dean Brackley, Sobrino was blessing and
thanking the many US citizens (Norteamericanos) who have
given so much of their lives to accompany the Salvadoran people
(also see "Maura, Ita, Dorothy, and Jean," in Chapter 2). It was
a surprising and moving development that the best of us should
be welcomed into the UCA's most symbolically sacred ground of
love and solidarity with the crucified people.

Dear Ellacu:

It is a contrivance to write to you, but perhaps this is a way to
tell ourselves what is important. And with that, I would like to
briefly set the stage on the anniversary of your martyrdom. I am
going to tell you about three things happening now that, as I
see them, have to do with what you were and what you spoke
about.

1. The "always" of the crucified people.

There is no longer much talk of "crucified peoples," as you and
Archbishop Romero put it, arriving at that brilliant formula
independently of one another, I believe, guided by the same
Salvadoran and Christian spirit. And even less do people insist
that this crucified people is "always" the sign of the times, as
you wrote from exile in Madrid. . . . The world is not getting
better, but rather remains gravely ill, as you said in your last
speech. What has gotten worse is honesty about reality, and the
"always" [of the crucified people] is not politically correct. But
there is no need to reverse course. Haiti and Somalia continue
to exist, and the new epidemic of homicide, between 12 and
15 murders a day in recent years, is the deadliest disease in our
country. "Light" alternatives increasingly influence our ways of
thinking and what is "politically correct" enslaves our language:

---

1. Lassalle-Klein, *Blood and Ink*, xix, 139, 146–147, 177–78.

"vulnerability," "under privileged," "developing countries." Nothing sounds bad. . . .

But I want to add, Ellacu, that there is another "always." There are many honest people who work so that the people who are "underwater"—I mean El Salvador—do not end up dying as "displaced" or "drowned" persons. Commitment and kindness also have their "always."

And once in a while a Dean Brackley emerges who, when they tell him that many people are praying for him, answers with all honesty: "Pray for those who have cancer and cannot get the medical attention that I have. And pray for those who have been left homeless and without food these days."

2. "What to do with the good ones?"

The question may seem strange, but it has been pressed upon me by the commotion caused by the National Court in Madrid.[2] Working so that those who are responsible for so many murders in this country, yours and those of two innocent women, should face trial is a very good and necessary thing. It can bring much

---

2. The Center for Justice and Accountability (CJA) reports, "On January 13, 2009, Judge Eloy Velasco, the judge of the Sixth Chamber of the Spanish National Court formally charged 14 former officers with murder, crimes against humanity and state terrorism for their role in the [Jesuit] massacre. Additionally, the judge reserved the right, during the course of the investigation, to charge former Salvadoran President and Commander of the Armed Forces Alfredo Cristiani for his role in covering up the crime. . . . On May 30, 2011, the Spanish National Court issued a 77-page indictment which added six new defendants to the original 14. The court also issued international arrest warrants through Interpol. In the charging document, Judge Velasco describes the far reaching conspiracy to kill the Jesuit priests and explains how it was conceived as a military operation at the highest levels of the Salvadoran military and the National Intelligence Directorate." CJA, "Foreign National Court," Murder of Jesuit Priests and Civilians in El Salvador/ The Jesuits Massacre Case. https://cja.org/what-we-do/litigation/the-jesuits-massacre-case/foreign-national-court-spain/.

good, and be an enormous and very necessary aid in bringing to an end, or mitigating, impunity.

Certainly, while it has not been on the news, we have been very happy that the Argentine military personnel who ordered the assassination of Bishop Enrique Angelelli in 1976 will be tried 35 years later. It is an example, a bit late in coming, that truth can triumph over a lie and a cover-up, which have millions of dollars and sophisticated weapons at their service. That justice can triumph over cruelty and depravity. And that the civilization of impunity, so close to the civilization of wealth against which you stubbornly warned us to the end, is a little impeded.

This situation notwithstanding, a question comes to my mind that may seem strange. Simply put, we seem to know what to do "with the bad guys," so that our actions, of course, produce good outcomes: establishing truth and justice in the country, offering forgiveness—although, more difficult than forgiving, is allowing yourself to be forgiven. And very good people are working on this.

We also know, at least in principle, what to do with the victims: which is what [the Third General Conference of Latin American Bishops at] Puebla says that God does for the poor, "coming to their defense and loving them." And these are absolutely not naive words, because coming to their defense inevitably involves getting into serious conflicts. It means entering "the struggle for justice," "the crucial struggle of our time," as stated by the 32nd General Congregation [of the Society of Jesus].

But, do we know what to do "with the good ones," with the saints? Certainly, to make them productive, to learn from them, their ideas and convictions, their ways of acting . . . And to thank them.

These last few days we are pressed to answer the question: what to do with Dean Brackley? We have kept vigil with and accompanied his body. Love and gratitude have overflowed in many celebrations with tears and joy in the journey to the cemetery.

But I am left with unease in regards to knowing what to do with Dean, with Archbishop Romero, with people like you. With Jesus of Nazareth. The answer is simple: to be like them, to follow them in what they do and in their way of being, to imitate them, historically, as you used to say. In short, to allow ourselves to be impacted by "the good ones" and the saints in what we do, and more deeply, in our way of being.

Understand me well, Ellacu. It is good and necessary to know how to respond to what the bad guys do, and to adequately react. A lot of people and institutions do this. But I think we should improve in reacting to the good ones, trying to be like them. Difficult? Certainly. But necessary in order to humanize this world. And also this church.

3. Dean Brackley

Ellacu, these words will sound familiar to you. "With Dean Brackley, God visited us." I think there is no greater confession of faith than to affirm that God continues to visit our world. It is the faith that most fills me. And since God is present in human beings, men and women, young and old, Salvadorans and Americans, martyrs and sinners, as was said before, the mystery unfolds in many convergent ways, and this is the greater mystery. God visited us in Archbishop Romero and in Dean. . . .

Dean, weeks before dying, spoke in his "Testimony of Gratitude"[3] of God's presence to him, with great humility, simplicity and lucidity. Now, using other more conceptual language, which I hope remains understandable, I want to speak to you about Dean [as he was] before God and with God.

The first thing is that Dean died drenched in God. That's how I see it, although one can only approach that mystery on tiptoes. In his last book, Dean tells of his problems with God, his frequent periods of agnosticism. It reminded me of your words

---

3. Dean Brackley, "Testimonio de gratitud del P. Dean Brackley," *Carta a las iglesias*, Año XXX, no. 618, 1–30 octubre 2011, 3.

of June 1969 that I have quoted many times: "Rahner bore his doubts about faith with elegance," and I thought something similar happened to you. But throughout the book, Dean offers his own faith, deep and simple, and very real. And readers are surprised to find the prologue written by the editor, [whose job it was] to judge the quality of the book. She describes herself as an agnostic, who didn't think much about the matter of God. But she confesses that, upon reading the text, her professional interest became an existential, personal interest. The text brought her to God, and Dean baptized her a year later. Struggling with God, like Jacob, or letting himself be seduced by God, like Jeremiah, Dean came to God. And he was drenched with God.

In that process, Dean confesses with immense gratitude that he met God in the poor. How many times did you write, Ellacu, that the poor are the place of the gospel and the place of God. And I also remember the words of Porfirio Miranda: "The problem is not finding God, but encountering him where He said he would be. In the poor." It is true that one does not always find God, being among the poor, since, among them and working for them, there are agnostics who are splendid human beings and who remain agnostics. But in the best tradition of Jesus, the God who one encounters among the poor has a special flavor. I think that mercy can make this flavor more exquisite, justice stronger, truth more incomparable, and fidelity more incalculable.

The Dean who was drenched with God was a remarkable example of a person who was interested in each and every one of the people with whom he lived and whom he encountered. Each and every one of them, Jesuit companions, family members, parishioners from Jayaque and the UCA, men and women, Salvadorans, North Americans and Europeans, and of course, the disinherited and insignificant, each had a very specific name and identity for him. Each one was unique. This gave his interactions with them a great quality. And it reminds me of the Jesus who knew all of his sheep by their names.

And his God was, in truth, the God of creation. Not because of any current trend, some of which are very good, Dean was very interested in women and feminism; in ecumenism, and was very friendly with people from other churches; in ecology; and I believe even in indigenous causes. But the fundamental arguments were neither categorical, nor taken from norms of the hierarchy or [Catholic] social teaching. I think for Dean the argument was that God is a God of all.

Dean reminded me of some words of Archbishop Romero that I have cited many times. They are from February 10, 1980, amid the barbarism that reigned in the country. He said, "Who will agree, dear brothers and sisters, that the fruit of my preaching should be that each one of us meets God and lives in the joy of his majesty and our littleness!" For Archbishop Romero, God did not dwarf humanity, but it was good for humanity to make itself small before God. This reminds me of Dean. He never put himself in the first place, nor did he talk about himself when things went well—"it was a success"—because he did it. He reminded me of Paul in his letter to the Corinthians [1 Cor 13:4-7]: "Love is patient, it is kind, love is not envious, it does not boast or become proud, it always apologizes, always trusts, always hopes, always perseveres." In this Dean reminded me of the great Father Arrupe. I believe he always thought of others before himself. He never worried if they would recognize the good he was doing. One does not often find this, which is why it surprises and impresses. And it helps us to avoid making ourselves into absolutes and to live our littleness with joy before God, as Archbishop Romero said.

One final thought. Dean did not die a martyr like you all did, but his last months were a martyrdom of the body due to the suffering caused by a very painful pancreatic cancer, and of the soul when he was assaulted by fears, feeling lonely, not remembered . . .

Father Dean did not die crucified, but he lived to the end actively participating in the crosses of this world. He worked with *power*, that is, with strength and energy, to take them [the crucified people] down from the cross. And he always thought of himself last. Like the crucified God.

Dean's last words are words of gratitude, [while feeling] basically lost, and unable to stand on solid ground. But gratitude lives from others and for others, from God and for God. Those who are grateful have the ability to make reality graceful. Ellacu, if you will allow me the expression—which I believe is a neologism—those who are grateful have the ability "to goodify reality" ["buenear la realidad"]. That is what Dean did.

Ellacu, you see that, in the midst of many evils and in spite of everything, we are happy. You all, Julia Elba and Celina, Jon Cortina and Father Ibisate, and now our dear Dean Brackley, have been with us. And through you, God has been with us. One cannot ask for more.

A hug, Jon
October 27, 2011
                              —"Letter to Ellacuría: The 'Always' of the Crucified People.
                                     'What to Do with the Good Ones.' Dean Brackley"
        "Carta a Ellacuría: El 'siempre' del pueblo crucificado. 'Qué hacer con los
                                              Buenos.' Dean Brackley," 25–27

Appendices

JON SOBRINO'S TRANSLATION OF ELLACURÍA'S THREE MOMENTS OF "FACING UP TO REAL THINGS AS REAL"

In 1975 Ellacuría wrote what may be his best-known article, "Toward a Foundation for Latin American Theological Method" ["Hacia una fundamentación del método teológico latino-americano"].[1] Ellacuría argues that "the formal structure of intelligence . . . is not to understand and grasp meaning, but to apprehend reality and to confront itself with that reality."[2] Here, Ellacuría first develops his three famous dimensions of "confronting oneself with real things as real": (1) "el hacerse cargo de la realidad;" (2) "el cargar con la realidad;" and (3) "el encargarse de la realidad." Early attempts to translate these phrases into English have been questioned by Sobrino and scholars at the UCA, which should not be considered surprising, given that they involve a difficult wordplay in Spanish.[3] In 2009, as

---

1. Ignacio Ellacuría, "Hacia una fundamentación del método teológico latino-americano," *ECA* 30, nos. 322–23 (August–September 1975): 409–25; see also Ellacuría, *Escritos teológicos*, I (San Salvador: UCA Editores, 2000), 187–218.

2. Ellacuría, "Hacia una fundamentación del método teológico latino-americano, 419–20; see also Ellacuría, *Escritos teológicos*, 207–208.

3. Kevin Burke's poetic early translation is perhaps best known: "realizing the weight of reality," "shouldering the weight of reality," and "taking charge of the weight of reality." In response, Dean Brackley asserts that Burke's "English rendering of these same three expressions, admittedly difficult, is . . . questionable." See Dean Brackley, Book Review, "Love That

editor for a Special Edition of Theological Studies on The Galilean Jesus,[4] I asked Sobrino to clarify his preferred translation for the three phrases, which appeared in the Spanish version of his article. Sobrino's preferred translation, which appears in his published article, is as follows: (1) "grasping what is at stake in reality;" (2) "assuming responsibility for reality and paying the price for it;" and (3) "taking charge of reality."[5] What follows is a section of a 2009 interview for a subsequent project, in which Sobrino reaffirms his position regarding the translation for these three phrases in question.

Lassalle-Klein: Jon, there continues to be some disagreement about how to translate into English Ellacuría's famous three moments: *"hacerse cargo de la realidad, cargar con la realidad, y encargarse de la realidad."* Can you tell me how you would translate them?

Sobrino: Yes, I did it already! The translation I did for the article that I wrote, and you published, in *Theological Studies* in June 2009, is how I would do it. I worked at it, and that's how I would do it. I took what you sent me and I made some changes in the translation, and this is how I would like to do it."

(1) "grasping what is at stake in reality;"

(2) "assuming responsibility for reality and paying the price for it;" and

(3) "taking charge of reality."

Lassalle-Klein: So, just to be sure, are you happy with the translation that appears there?

Produces Hope: The Thought of Ignacio Ellacuría. Edited by Kevin F. Burke and Robert Lassalle-Klein," *Theological Studies* 68 (2007): 934.

4. Lassalle-Klein, *The Galilean Jesus*, Special Issue, *Theological Studies* 70, no. 2 (2009).

5. Sobrino, "Jesus of Galilee from the Salvadoran Context: Compassion, Hope, and Following the Light of the Cross," *The Galilean Jesus*, Special Issue, *Theological Studies* 70, no. 2 (2009): 449.

Sobrino: Yes, that's it! I'm very happy with that translation.
—Robert Lassalle-Klein, Interview with Jon Sobrino at Santa Clara
University Jesuit Community, November 4, 2009, 5:30–6:15 p.m.

LETTER TO FR. KOLVENBACH, S.J., EXPLAINING NONADHERENCE TO "NOTIFICATION" FROM THE CONGREGATION FOR THE DOCTRINE OF THE FAITH

November 26, 2006, the Congregation for the Doctrine of the Faith (CDF), issued a "Notification," warning of "certain imprecisions and errors" (Notification, #1) in Jon Sobrino's two-volume Christology, published a few years earlier (1991 and 1999). Two weeks later, Sobrino wrote the following letter to Fr. Peter Hans Kolvenbach, S.J., Superior General of the Society of Jesus, explaining why he could not, in good conscience, sign a statement that he adhered "without reservations" to the criticisms stated in the "Notification."

The letter is a remarkably personal expression of pain and hope from one of the most important Catholic theologians of the twentieth century to what many commentators regard as an unfair campaign of harassment against Fr. Sobrino by forces in the church hierarchy hostile to Latin American liberation theology. While unofficial versions of this letter were previously leaked to the press, the following text of his letter was delivered directly to me by Sobrino, who wishes to see it published under his name. Readers will be interested to learn that, despite warnings by the CDF issued under previous popes of potentially "dangerous" propositions in the writings of many Latin American liberation theologians, and Fr. Sobrino in particular, Pope Francis has brought a new appreciation to the Vatican for their work and its emphasis on the "preferential option for the poor." On November 14, 2015, Sobrino was invited to an important Vatican conference, after which Pope Francis personally greeted Fr. Sobrino and strongly encouraged him to "keep writing."

The letter readily acknowledges an error, which is "technical, not doctrinal," in Sobrino's interpretation of one aspect of classical Christian doctrine (the 'comunicatio idiomatum'), while complaining that he does "not recognize" his writing in the descriptions provided by the Notification. It is worth noting that the overwhelming consensus among theologians and bishops is that Sobrino's two volumes stand "well within the mainstream"[6] of Catholic theological reflection on the tradition of the church. Such writers tend to describe the "Notification" as a distorted reading of Sobrino's writings articulating (1) honest criticisms of Fr. Sobrino's writings from the perspective of a minority of cardinals and theologians, some of whom still favor the neo-Thomistic Christology that dominated seminary education a generation ago (now a minority position); and/or (2) an unfortunate, and ultimately unsuccessful, attempt by some within the church hierarchy to distort, and thereby discredit, some of the central insights of Latin American liberation theology.

December 13, 2006

Dear P. Kolvenbach:

Before anything else, thank you for the letter you wrote to me on November 20 and for all the steps you have taken to defend my writings and me as a person. Fr. Idiáquez told me to write to you about my position regarding the notification and the reasons why I do not adhere—"without reservations," as you say in your letter—to them [the conclusions stated there]. In the brief text that follows, I will explain my reaction to the notification, because, as you say, it is normal for the news to appear in the media and because theological colleagues will be waiting for a word from me.

---

6. William Loewe, "Interpreting the Notification: Christological Issues," in Stephen J. Pope, ed., *Hope and Solidarity: Jon Sobrino's Challenge to Christian Theology* (Maryknoll, NY: Orbis Books, 2008), 146.

The Fundamental Reason

The fundamental reason [for my position] is as follows. A good number of theologians read my two books before the publication of the text of the Congregation [for the Doctrine] of the Faith [CDF] in 2004. Several of them also read the text of the Congregation. Their unanimous opinion is that there is nothing in my two books that is not compatible with the faith of the Church.

The first book, *Jesus Christ Liberator: A Historical-Theological Reading of Jesus of Nazareth*, was published fifteen years ago in 1991 in Spanish, and has been translated into Portuguese, English, German and Italian. The Portuguese translation has the imprimatur of Cardinal Arns, dated December 4, 1992. As far as I know, no review or oral theological commentary questioned my doctrine.

The text of the second book, *Faith in Jesus Christ: An Essay from the Victims*, was published seven years ago in 1999, and has been translated into Portuguese, English and Italian. It was very carefully examined before its publication by several theologians, in some cases by order of the Provincial, Adam Cuadra, and in others, at my request. They are the Frs. J. I. González Faus, J. Vives and X. Alegre, of San Cugat; Fr. Carlo Palacio, from Bello Horizonte; Fr. Gesteira, from Comillas; Fr. Javier Vitoria, of Deusto; Fr. Martin Maier, from *Stimmen der Zeit*. Several of them are experts in dogmatic theology, one, in exegesis, and another, in patristics.

Recently in 2005, Father Sesboué, at the request of Martin Maier, was kind enough to read the second book, *Faith in Jesus Christ*, having also read, as I understand, the 2004 text of the Congregation of the [Doctrine of the] Faith. Father Maier asked him to focus on whether there was something in my book against the faith of the Church. His fifteen-page answer as a whole is laudatory of the book, and he did not find anything to criticize from the point of view of faith. He found just one error, which he calls technical, not doctrinal. "My intention is to show the center of gravity of the work and how seriously it takes the conciliar affirmations, like the titles of Christ in the NT. I found only one real error, its interpretation of the communication of attributes [the *comunicatio idiomatum*], but it is a technical non-doctrinal error." (I affirm from now on that I do not have any problem in clarifying, to the extent of my possibilities, that technical error).

Regarding the Congregation's way of analyzing my text, he says the following: "I did not want to respond with too much precision to the document of the CDF which also takes aim at Sobrino's first book and seems to me so exaggerated that it is worthless. Talleyrand had this to say: 'What is exaggerated is insignificant!' With a deliberately suspicious method like this, I can find many heresies in the encyclicals of John Paul II! I did consider this point [about the first book] in my assessment. I want to say that this book seems to me more rigorous in its formulations than the previous one. I have also cited texts from the tradition, contemporaries, and even popes who go in the direction of Sobrino (in that regard I use the method of the CDF!)" I also gave a copy of the text of Fr. Sesboué, Fr. Idiáquez and Fr. Valentín Menéndez. All these theologians are well acquainted with christology, at the theological and doctrinal level. They are responsible people. They have explicitly focused on [finding] possible doctrinal errors in my work. They are respectful of the Church. And they have not found doctrinal errors or dangerous claims. For that reason, I cannot understand how the notification reads my texts in such a different and even contrary manner.

This is the first and fundamental reason for not signing on to the notification: "I do not feel [accurately] represented at all in the overall judgment of the notification." For this reason, I do not think it is honest to sign it. Moreover, it would amount to a lack of respect for the aforementioned theologians.

Thirty Years of Relations with the Hierarchy

The 2004 document and the notification are not a total surprise. Since 1975 I have had to answer to the Congregation for Catholic Education, under Cardinal Garrone in 1976, and to the Congregation [for the Doctrine] of the Faith, first under Cardinal Seper and then, several times, under Cardinal Ratzinger. Father Arrupe, above all, but also Father Vincent O'Keefe as vicar general, and Father Paolo Dezza as papal delegate, always encouraged me to respond with honesty, fidelity and humility. They thanked me for my positive willingness to respond and they made me understand that the Vatican curias were not always distinguished by being honest and very gospel-centered. My experience, then, comes from far away. And you know what has happened here during the years of your generalate.

What I want to add now is that not only have I had serious warnings and accusations from these congregations, especially that of the [Congregation for the Doctrine of the] Faith, but from early on an environment was created in the Vatican, in several diocesan curias, and among several bishops, that was against of my theology—and in general, against the theology of liberation. An atmosphere was created of opposition to my theology, a priori, without the need in many cases to read my writings. There are thirty long years of history, so I am just going to mention some significant facts. I do so, not because this comprises a fundamental reason for not signing on to the notification, but to [help you] understand the situation in which we find ourselves, and how difficult it is, at least for me, even doing my best, to address the problem honestly, humanely and evangelically. And to be honest, though I have already said that this is not a reason not to adhere to the notification, I feel that it is not ethical for me to "approve or support" with my signature a way of proceeding that has little of the gospel, and which has structural dimensions, by one measure, that are quite widespread. I think that endorsing these procedures does nothing to help the Church of Jesus, to present the face of God in our world, to encourage the following of

Jesus, or for the "crucial struggle of our time," faith and justice. I say this with great humility.

Some facts regarding the generalized climate that has been created against my theology, beyond the accusations of the congregations, are as follows.

Archbishop Romero wrote in his diary on May 3, 1979: "I visited Fr. López Gall. . . . He told me, as a friend, of the negative judgment in some sectors towards the theological writings of Jon Sobrino." As for Archbishop Romero, a few months later he asked if I would write for him the speech he gave at the University of Louvain on February 2, 1980,—in 1977 I had already written for him the second pastoral letter, "The Church, Body of Christ in the History."

I wrote the Louvain speech. He liked it a lot, he read it in its entirety, and he thanked me. Before his change as a [arch]bishop, Bishop Romero had accused me of doctrinal hazards, which shows that he knew how to move in this problematic environment (he also wrote a critical judgment against Ellacuría's "*Freedom Made Flesh*" [*Teología política*] in 1974). But later, he never warned me of such dangers. I think my theology seemed to him doctrinally correct—at least in substance. (I know very well that my possible influence on his writings and homilies has been a problem in the Vatican for his canonization. I wrote a text of some twenty pages about them, and I signed it).

When Alfonso López Trujillo was named a cardinal, he told a group shortly thereafter, more or less publically, that he was going to do away with Gustavo Gutiérrez, Leonardo Boff, Ronaldo Muñoz and Jon Sobrino. That's what I was told, and it seems very plausible to me. The stories about López Trujillo concerning Fr. Ellacuría—Archbishop Romero, above all—and me, are endless. They continue to this day, and they started soon. I believe that in 1976 or 1977 he spoke against the theologies of Ellacuría and me at a meeting of the Episcopal Conference of El Salvador, to which he invited himself. Later, in a letter to

Ellacuría, he emphatically denied that he had ever talked about us at that conference. But we had the firsthand testimony of Bishop Rivera, who was present at the meeting of the episcopal conference.

In 1983, Cardinal Corripio, archbishop of Mexico, banned the celebration of a theological congress organized by the Passionists to celebrate, according to their charism, the year of redemption, which was being sponsored by John Paul II. They wanted a theological treatment of the theme of the cross of Christ and our peoples. They invited me and I accepted. Later they told me about the cardinal's ban. The reason, or an important reason, was that I was going to give two talks at the congress.

In Honduras, the archbishop scolded a group of sisters because they had gone to a nearby diocese to a conference of mine. The bishop had invited me. I think his name was Bishop Corrivau, a Canadian.

Just one more example so as not to tire you. In 1987 or 1988, more or less, I received an invitation to speak to a large group of laity in Argentina, in the diocese of Bishop Hesayne. It was about the revitalization of Christians who had suffered during the dictatorship. And I accepted. Shortly afterwards I received a letter from Bishop Hesayne telling me that my visit to his diocese had been a subject of debate at a meeting of the Episcopal Conference.

Cardinal Primatesta said that he thought it was very bad that I was going to speak in Argentina. Bishop Hesayne, defended me as a person and defended my orthodoxy. He asked the cardinal if he had read any of my books, and he admitted that he had not. Nonetheless, the bishop was forced to cancel the invitation. He wrote to me and apologized with great affection and humility, and asked me to understand the situation. I replied that I understood and thanked him.

Regarding what I have said about Argentina, I am certain. What follows I heard from two priests, I do not know if they were from Argentina or Bolivia, who passed through the UCA. When they saw me, they told me they knew about what had happened in Argentina. In short, they told Bishop Hesayne at the meeting of the Episcopal Conference that he had to choose: either he invited Jon Sobrino to his diocese and the Pope would not come on his next visit to Argentina, or he would welcome the Pope to his diocese and Jon Sobrino could not visit.

I do not want to wear you out, but believe me, I could tell more stories. There are also bishops who have opposed my giving lectures in Spain. I do not think this "bad reputation" was something specifically personal, but part of the campaign against the theology of liberation.

And now I will state my second reason for not adhering [to the conclusions of the notification]. It has to do less with the documents of the Congregation [for the Doctrine] of the Faith, and more with the Vatican's way of proceeding during the last twenty or thirty years. In these years, many male and female theologians, good people, with limitations of course, with love for Jesus Christ and the Church, and with great love for the poor, have been mercilessly persecuted. And not only them. Also bishops, as you know, Archbishop Romero when he was alive (there are still those in the Vatican who do not like him, at least they do not like the real Archbishop Romero, but rather a watered down Archbishop Romero), Don Helder Camara after his death, and Proaño, Don Samuel Ruiz, and a very long etcetera. They have tried to decapitate CLAR [the Confederation of Latin American Religious], sometimes with chicanery, and thousands of religious women and men of immense generosity, which is all the more painful due to the humility of many of them. And above all, they have done everything possible to make basic Christian communities disappear, the small ones, the privileged ones of God.

Adhering to the notification, which is largely an expression of that campaign and its way of proceeding, often clearly unjust, against so many good people, I feel would be to endorse it. I do not want to commit the sin of arrogance, but I do not think this would help the cause of the poor of Jesus and the Church of the poor.

Criticisms of My Theology by Joseph Ratzinger, the Theologian

I believe this topic is important in order to understand where we are, although it is not a reason not to sign the notification.

Shortly before publishing the first *Instruction on Some Aspects of the "Theology of Liberation,"* they ran a text about this theology, in manuscript form, by Cardinal Joseph Ratzinger. Father César Jerez, then Provincial, received the text from a Jesuit friend from the United States. The text was published later in *30 giorni* III/3 (1984) pp. 48–55. I was able to read it, already published, in *Il Regno, Documenti* 21 (1984) pp. 220–223. This article mentions the names of four liberation theologians: Gustavo Gutiérrez, Hugo Assmann, Ignacio Ellacuría, and mine, which is the most frequently cited. I quote verbatim what he says about me. The references are from my book *Jesus in Latin America, His Meaning for Faith and Christology* (Maryknoll, NY: Orbis Books, 1987); *Jesús en América Latina. Su significado para le fe y la cristología* (San Salvador: UCA Editores, 1982) [Editor: all translations in this text are mine, but page numbers from the 1987 Orbis translation and from 1982 Spanish original are provided in that order with each citation].

a) *Ratzinger*: "Regarding the faith, for example, J. Sobrino says: The experience that Jesus has of God is radically historical. 'His faith becomes fidelity.' Sobrino fundamentally replaces, therefore, faith with 'fidelity to history' (Fidelity to history, pp. 126; 143–144)."

Commentary. What I say verbatim is: "His faith in the mystery of God becomes fidelity to that mystery". . . with which I want to emphasize the evolving nature of the act of faith. I also say that "the letter (to the Hebrews) admirably summarizes how historical fidelity is found in Jesus, and how practice of love for people and fidelity to the mystery of God is found in history, (p. 126; 144). Ratzinger's interpretation of replacing faith with fidelity to history is unjustified. I repeat several times: "fidelity to the mystery of God."

b) *Ratzinger:* "'Jesus is faithful to the deep conviction that the mystery of human life . . . is really what is ultimate.' (p. 127; 144). Here a fusion is produced between God and history, which allows Sobrino to keep the [fifth century] Chalcedonian formula with respect to Jesus, but with a totally altered sense: one can see how the classical criteria of orthodoxy are not applicable to the analysis of this theology."

Commentary. What my text says is that "history makes his fidelity to God credible, and his fidelity to God, to the one who appointed him, engenders his fidelity to history, to living 'on behalf of others'" (p. 127, 144). I do not confuse God and history at all. Furthermore, fidelity is not to a history that is abstract, far from God and absolutized, rather it is a fidelity to love one's sisters and brothers, which has a specific kind of ultimacy in the New Testament and mediates the reality of God.

c) *Ratzinger:* "Ignacio Ellacuría hints at this fact on the cover of the book with this statement: Sobrino 'says again . . . that Jesus is God, immediately adding however that the true God is only the one who reveals himself historically and scandalously in Jesus and in the poor, who continue his presence. Only those who hold these two statements in tension and together are orthodox . . .'"

Commentary. I do not see what is wrong with Ellacuría's words.

d) *Ratzinger:* "The fundamental concept of Jesus' preaching is the 'Kingdom of God.' This concept is also found in the core of liberation theologies, but read against the background of Marxist hermeneutics. According to J. Sobrino the kingdom should not be understood in a spiritualistic way, neither universalistically, nor in the sense of an abstract eschatological reserve. It should be understood in a factional and praxis-oriented way.

Only beginning from the praxis of Jesus, and not theoretically, can we define the meaning of the kingdom; working with the historical reality that surrounds us in order to transform it into the Kingdom" (pp. 142–143; 166).

Commentary. It is untrue that I speak of the kingdom of God against the background of Marxist hermeneutics. Yes, it is true that I give decisive importance to reproducing the praxis of Jesus to obtain a concept that can bring us closer to the one that Jesus had. But the latter is a problem of philosophical epistemology, which also has roots in the biblical understanding of what it is to know. As Jeremiah and Hosea say: "To do justice, is not this to know me?"

e) *Ratzinger:* "In this context I would also like to mention the impressive, but ultimately shocking, interpretation of death and resurrection by J. Sobrino. He asserts, first of all, against universally held conceptions, that the resurrection is primarily a hope of the crucified, who comprise the majority of humanity: all those millions on whom structural injustice is imposed like a slow crucifixion (p. 151; 176). The believer also takes part in the reign of Jesus over history through the implantation of the Kingdom [of God], that is, in the struggle for justice and integral liberation, in the transformation of unjust structures into more human structures. This lordship over history is put into practice, to the extent that the act of God that raises Jesus is repeated in history, that is, giving life to the crucified [peoples] of history (p. 156; 181). The human person takes over the acts of God, and in this can be seen the transformation of the biblical message in an almost tragic way, if one thinks about how this attempt to imitate God has been, and is being carried out."

Commentary. If the resurrection of Jesus is that of a crucified person, it seems at least plausible to theologically understand [the meaning of] hope first for the crucified. We can "all" participate in this hope to the extent that we participate in the cross. And the phrase, "repeating the gesture of God in history" is obviously metaphorical language, which has nothing to do with hubris and arrogance. It echoes the ideal of Jesus: "be good in all things as the heavenly Father is good."

Thus far [I have presented] commentary on Ratzinger's accusations. I do not recognize my theology in this reading of the texts. Moreover, as you will remember, Fr. Alfaro wrote a judgment in his article, "Analysis of the book, 'Jesus in Latin America' by Jon Sobrino," *Revista Latinoamericana de Teología* 1 , 1984, pp. 103–120) about the book from which Ratzinger takes his quotations, without finding any error. As far as orthodoxy is concerned, it concludes verbatim:

a) express and repeated affirmation of faith in the divinity (divine sonship) of Christ throughout the entire book;

b) believing recognition of the normative and binding character of the christological dogmas, defined by the ecclesial magisterium in the ecumenical councils;

c) faith in Christian eschatology, already begun now in the historical present as an anticipation of its coming meta-historical fulfillment (beyond death);

d) faith in Christian liberation as "integral liberation," that is, as the total salvation of humanity in its interiority and corporality, in its relationship to God, to others, to death and to the world. These four truths of the Christian faith are fundamental for all Christology. Sobrino affirms them without any ambiguity (pp.117–18).

And it is bad that, without mentioning my name, the *Instruction* of 1984, (IX. "The Theological Application of This Core"), repeats some ideas that Ratzinger thinks he has found in my book. "Some go so far as to identify God Himself with history and to define faith as 'fidelity to history'" (# 4).

I believe that in 1984 Cardinal Ratzinger did not fully understand the theology of liberation, nor does he seem to have accepted the critical reflections of Juan Luis Segundo in *Teología de la liberación. Respuesta al Cardenal Ratzinger*, Madrid, 1985 [*Theology and the Church: A Response to Cardinal Ratzinger and a Warning to the Whole Church*, Winston Press, 1985], and of I. Ellacuría, "Estudio teológico-pastoral de la Instrucción sobre algunos aspectos de 'la teología de la liberación,'" *Revista Latinoamericana de Teología* 2, 1984, pp. 145–178 [*Escritos teológicos*, I, 397–449]. Personally, I think that even today it is difficult to understand [his position]. And a commentary that I have read on at least two occasions has disgusted me. It is not very objective and can go as far as being unfair. The idea is that "what (some) liberation theologians seek is to achieve fame, to attract attention."

I am done. It is not easy to dialogue with the Congregation [for the Doctrine] of the Faith. Sometimes it seems impossible. It seems obsessed with finding any limitation or error, or for taking as such what might simply be a different conceptualization of some truth of the faith. In my opinion, this represents, to a large extent, ignorance, prejudice and an obsession to put an end to the theology of liberation. Sincerely, it is not easy to dialogue with that kind of mentality.

How many times have I recalled the presupposition of the Spiritual Exercises of St. Ignatius: "Every good Christian should be more ready to put a good interpretation on the statement of their neighbor than to condemn it as false." And I recently read in the press a paragraph from the forthcoming book of Benedict XVI about Jesus of Nazareth.

> It goes without saying that this book is in no way an exercise of the magisterium, but is solely an expression of my personal search "for the face of the Lord" (cf. Ps 27:8). Everyone is free, then, to contradict me. I would only ask my readers for that initial goodwill without which there can be no understanding [*Jesus of Nazareth*, xxiii–xxiv].

Personally, I offer the Pope sympathy and understanding. And I vehemently wish that the Congregation [for the Doctrine] of the Faith would treat male and female theologians the same way.

Important Background Problems

In my March 2005 response, I tried to explain my thinking, which has been in vain. For that reason I am not going to comment now, once again, on the accusations that the notification makes against me, since fundamentally they are the same. I just want to mention some important issues, on which we could reflect in the future.

1. The poor as a place to do theology. This is a problem of theological epistemology, demanded, or at least suggested, by Scripture. Personally, I do not doubt that reality is better seen, and that the revelation of God is better understood from [the place of] the poor.

2. The mystery of Christ always inundates us. I maintain as fundamental that Christ is a sacrament of God, a presence of God in our world. And I maintain as equally fundamental that Christ is a specific human and historical being. Docetism[7] seems to me to remain the greatest danger to our faith.

3. The constitutive relationality of Jesus with the kingdom of God. In the simplest possible words, this is a world as God wants it to be, in which there is justice and peace, respect and dignity, and in which the poor are the center of interest for believers and churches. Likewise, the constitutive relationality of Jesus with a God who is Father, in whom he totally trusts, and in a Father who is God to whom he makes himself totally available.

4. Jesus is the son of God, the word made *sarx*. And in this I see the central mystery of the faith: *transcendence* has

---

7. "The view that Jesus was a divine being who only appeared to be human." "Docetism," *Oxford Biblical Studies Online*. http://www.oxford-biblicalstudies.com/article/opr/t94/e544.

become *trans-descendance* in order to get to *con-descendance* [*descendance-with*].

5. Jesus brings the definitive salvation, truth, and love of God. He makes it present through his life, praxis, prophetic denunciation and utopian annunciation, cross, and resurrection. And [the Third General Conference of Latin American Bishops at] Puebla, referring to Matthew 25, affirms Christ "has wanted to identify himself with special tenderness with the weakest and poorest" (No. 196). *Ubi pauperes ibi Christus.*

6. Many other things are important in the faith. I just want to mention one more, which John XXIII and Cardinal Lercaro proclaimed at Vatican II: The Church as "Church of the poor." A Church of true compassion, of prophecy to defend the oppressed, and of utopia to give them hope.

7. And in a seriously ill world like the current one, I advance as utopia the idea of that "*extra pauperes nulla salus*" [outside the poor there is no salvation].

Of these and many other topics, we must speak more slowly. I think it is good that we all dialogue. Personally, I am willing to do it.

Dear Father Kolvenbach, this is what I wanted to communicate to you. You should know that, while these things are unpleasant, I can say that I am at peace. This comes from the memory of countless men and women who were friends, many of them martyrs. These days, the memory of Fr. Jon Cortina brings me joy again. If you will permit me to speak with total sincerity, I do not feel "at home" in this world of curia, diplomacy, calculations, power, etc. Being far from "that world," even though I did not seek that, does not cause me distress. If I am understood, it even gives me relief.

I do feel that the notification will produce some suffering. To put it simply, my friends and family, a sister I have who was very close to Archbishop Romero and the martyrs. I also think that it will make life more difficult, for example, for my great friend Fr. Rafael de Sivatte. If he does not already have a few problems in maintaining a serious Department of Theology, which he keeps up very well through his great capacity, dedication and scholarship—he will now have to find another professor of Christology, and, as you know, he will also have to find another professor of Church History, since, unjustly, Fr. Rodolfo Cardenal is not going to teach, because he is not viewed well by the local hierarchy.

I do not know if this long letter will help you in your conversations with the Vatican. I hope that it will. I have tried to be as sincere as possible. And I thank you for all the efforts you have made to defend us.

I remember you with affection before the Lord.
Jon Sobrino

—Jon Sobrino, *Letter to Fr. Peter Hans Kolvenbach*;
translated by Robert Lassalle-Klein

Works Cited

Alfaro, Juan. "Análisis del libro 'Jesús en América latina' de Jon Sobrino." *Revista Latinoamericana de Teología* (1984): 103–20.

Benedict XVI, Pope. *Jesus of Nazareth: From the Baptism in the Jordan to the Transfiguration.* New York: Doubleday, 2007.

Boff, Leonardo. *Jesucristo el liberador.* Santander, Spain: Sal Terrae, 1985. *Jesus Christ Liberator,* Maryknoll, NY: Orbis Books, 1978.

Brackley, Dean. "Book Review. *Love That Produces Hope*: The Thought of Ignacio Ellacuría. Edited by Kevin F. Burke and Robert Lassalle-Klein." *Theological Studies* 68 (2007): 932–34.

———. "Testimonio de gratitud del P. Dean Brackley." *Carta a las Iglesias.* Año XXX, No. 618, 1–30 de octubre de 2011: 3.

Budi, Hartono. "The Christology of Jon Sobrino and Contemporary Martyrdom." Th.D. Thesis. Graduate Theological Union & Jesuit School of Theology at Berkeley, 1999. Included in an appendix: "Carta a Hartono Budi." San Salvador-Berkeley, CA. 30 de junio 1999.

Burke, Kevin, and Lassalle-Klein, Robert, eds. *Love That Produces Hope: The Thought of Ignacio Ellacuría.* Collegeville, MN: Liturgical Press, 2006.

Casaldáliga, Pedro. "The 'Crucified' Indians—A Case of Anonymous Collective Martyrdom." *Concilium* 163 (1983): 48–52.

———. "Salmo de abril en Sao Paulo." *El tiempo y la espera.* Santander: Sal Terrae, 1986.

Casas, Bartolomé de las. *Historia de las Indias.* In Tudela Bueso, J. Pérez de, eds. *Obras Escogidas,* 5 vols. Vol 2. Madrid, 1957–58.

Catechism of the Catholic Church. Libreria Editrice Vaticana, Citta del Vaticano, 1993. http://www.vatican.va/archive/ENG0015/_INDEX.HTM#fonte.

Center for Justice and Accountability. "Foreign National Court"/"Murder of Jesuit Priests and Civilians in El Salvador/The Jesuits Massacre Case." https://cja.org/what-we-do/litigation/the-jesuits-massacre-case/foreign-national-court-spain/.

Congregation for the Doctrine of the Faith. "Instruction on Certain Aspects of the *Theology of Liberation*." August 6, 1984. http://www.vatican.va/roman_curia/congregations/cfaith/documents/rc_con_cfaith_doc_19840806_theology-liberation_en.html.

———. "Notification on the Works of Father Jon Sobrino, S.J.: *Jesucristo liberador. Lectura histórico de Jesús de Nazaret* (Madrid: 1991) and *La fe en Jesucristo. Ensayo desde las víctimas* (San Salvador, 1999)." November 26, 2006. http://www.vatican.va/roman_curia/congregations/cfaith/documents/rc_con_cfaith_doc_20061126_notification-sobrino_en.html.

———. "Explanatory Note on the Notification on the Works of Father Jon Sobrino, S.J." November 26, 2006. http://www.vatican.va/roman_curia/congregations/cfaith/documents/rc_con_cfaith_doc_20061126_nota-sobrino_en.html.

Consejo Episcopal Latinoamericano. *La evangelización en el presente y en el futuro de America Latina / III Conferencia General del Episcopado Latinoamericano. Puebla de los Angeles, 27 de enero–13 de febrero de 1979.*

Elizondo, Miguel. "La Primera Semana como comienzo indispensable de conversión," 3. "Reunión-Ejercicios de la vice-provincia Jesuitica de Centroamérica, Diciembre 1969," 4–8. *Reflexion teológico-espiritual de la Compañía de Jesús en Centroamérica, II.* San Salvador: Archives of the Society of Jesus, Central American Province. *Survey S.J. de Centroamérica.* Diciembre 1969.

Ellacuría, Ignacio. "Aporte de la teología de la liberación a las religiones abrahámicas en la superación del individualismo y del positivismo." *Revista Latinoamericana de Teología* 10 (1987): 3–28.

————. "The Crucified People." *Mysterium Liberationis: Fundamental Concepts of Liberation Theology*. Ellacuría, Ignacio, and Sobrino, Jon, eds. Maryknoll, NY: Orbis Books, 1993, 580–603.

————. "Discernir *el signo* de los tiempos." *Escritos teológicos*, 2:133–35.

————. "El desafío de las mayorías pobres." *ECA* 493–94 (1989): 1075–80.

————. *Escritos teológicos*, 4 vols. San Salvador: UCA, 2000–2002.

————. "Estudio teológico-pastoral de la Instrucción sobre algunos aspectos de 'la teología de la liberación.'" *Revista Latinoamericana de Teología* 2 (1984): 145–78. Also in *Escritos teológicos*, vol. 1. San Salvador: UCA Editores, 2000, 397–449.

————. *Freedom Made Flesh: The Mission of Christ and His Church*. Drury, John, trans. Maryknoll, NY: Orbis Books, 1976. *Teología política*. San Salvador: Ediciónes del Secretaridado Sociál Interdiocesano, 1973.

————. "Hacía una fundamentación filosófica del método teológico latinoamericano." *Estudios Centroamericanos* 50 (1975): 409–25. Also in *Escritos teológicos*, vol. 1. San Salvador: UCA Editores, 2000, 187–218.

————. "The Kingdom of God and Unemployment in the Third World." *Concilium* 160 (1982): 91–96.

————. "Lectura latinoamericana de los Ejercicios Espirituales de San Ignacio." *Revista Latinoamericana de Teología* 23 (1991): 111–47.

————. "El pueblo crucificado, ensayo de soteriología histórica." *Escritos teológicos*, vol. 2. San Salvador: UCA Editores, 2000, 137–70.

————. "El Reino de Dios y el paro en el tercer mundo." *Concilium* 180 (1982): 588–96.

————. *Quinto Centenario América Latina. Descubrimiento o encubrimento?* Barcelona: Cuadernos Cristianisme i Justicia, 1990.

————. "La superación del reduccionismo idealista en Zubiri." *Escritos filosóficos*, vol. 3, 403. Reprinted from *Estudios Centroamericanos* no. 477 (1988): 633–50.

————. "La teología como momento ideológico de la praxis eclesial." *Estudios Eclesiásticos* 53 (1978): 457–76.

————. "Teología en un mundo sufriente: La teología de la liberación como 'intellectus amoris.'" *Revista Latinoamericana de Teología* 15 (1988): 243–66.

————. "Utopía y profetismo desde América Latina." *ECA* 17 (1989): 141–84. Translation, "Utopia and Prophecy in Latin America." *Mysterium Liberationis*, 289–328.

Ellacuría, Ignacio, and Sobrino, Jon. *Mysterium Liberationis: Fundamental Concepts of Liberation Theology*. Maryknoll, NY: Orbis Books, 1993.

Fleming, S.J., David L., *The Spiritual Exercises of Saint Ignatius: A Literal Translation and a Contemporary Reading*. St. Louis: Institute of Jesuit Sources, 1978.

Gutiérrez, Gustavo. *The Power of the Poor in History*. Maryknoll, NY: Orbis Books, 1983.

————. "Speaking about God." *Concilium* 171 (February 1984): 27–31.

Lassalle-Klein, Robert. *Blood and Ink: Ignacio Ellacuría, Jon Sobrino, and the Jesuit Martyrs of the University of Central America*. Maryknoll, NY: Orbis Books, 2014.

————. Interview with Jon Sobrino by Robert Lassalle-Klein, Santa Clara, CA, March 17, 1994. Transcript in personal files of Robert Lassalle-Klein.

————. Interview with Jon Sobrino by Robert Lassalle-Klein, San Salvador, April 19, 1994. Transcript in personal files of Robert Lassalle-Klein.

————. Interview with Jon Sobrino, S.J by Robert Lassalle-Klein, July 5, 1994. Transcript in personal files of Robert Lassalle-Klein.

————. Interview with Jon Sobrino at Santa Clara University Jesuit Community. November 4, 2009, 5:30–6:15 p.m. Transcript in personal files of Robert Lassalle-Klein.

————, ed. *Jesus of Galilee: Contextual Christology for the 21st Century*. Maryknoll, NY: Orbis Books, 2011.

Lassalle-Klein, Robert, and Kevin Burke, eds. *Love That Produces Hope: The Thought of Ignacio Ellacuría*. Collegeville, MN: Liturgical Press, 2006.

Lassalle-Klein, Robert, with Elizondo, Virgilio, and Gutiérrez, Gustavo, eds. *The Galilean Jesus*. Special Issue of *Theological Studies* 70, no. 2 (Spring 2009).

Rahner, Karl. *The Church and the Sacraments*. O'Hara, W. J., trans. London: Burns and Oates, 1963 [1961].

————. *Faith in a Wintry Season: Conversations & Interviews with Karl Rahner in the Last Years of His Life*. Herder & Herder, 1989.

————. "History of the World and Salvation History." *Theological Investigations*. London: Darton, Longman and Todd, 1966, 5:97–114.

————. *On the Theology of Death*. Henkey, Charles H., trans. London: Burns and Oates, 1961 [1958].

————. "Remarks on the Theological Treatise de Trinitate." *Theological Investigations*. London: Darton, Longman and Todd, 1966, 4:77–102.

————. "The Theology of the Symbol." *Theological Investigations*. London: Darton, Longman and Todd, 1966, 4:223–52.

Rahner, Karl, Paul Imhof, and Hubert Biallowons, eds. Egan, Harvey D., trans. *Faith in a Wintry Season: Conversation and Interactions with Karl Rahner in the Last Years of His Life*. New York: Crossroad, 1990.

————. *Karl Rahner in Dialogue: Conversations and Interviews 1965–1982*. New York: Crossroad, 1986.

Rahner, Karl, and Weger, Karl-Heinz. *Our Christian Faith: Answers for the Future*. McDonagh, Francis, trans. New York: Crossroad, 1981.

Rickaby, S.J., Joseph. *The Spiritual Exercises of St. Ignatius Loyola. Spanish and English*. London: Burns and Oates, 1915.

Romero, Archbishop Oscar. "Homilía en Aguilares [June 19, 1977]." In Sobrino, J., et al., eds. *La voz de los sin voz: La palabra viva de Monseñor Oscar Arnulfo Romero*, 207–12.

———. "Second Pastoral Letter: The Church, the Body of Christ in History." In *Voice of the Voiceless: The Four Pastoral Letters and Other Statements*. Maryknoll, NY: Orbis Books, 1985, 63–84. Sobrino, Jon; Martín-Baro, I., Cardenal, R., eds. Walsh, Michael J., trans. *La voz de los sin voz. La palabra viva de Monseñor Romero*. San Salvador, UCA Editores, 1980.

Segundo, Juan Luis. *Teología de la liberación. Respuesta al Cardenal Ratzinger*. Madrid, 1985. Diercksmeier, John W., trans. *Theology and the Church: A Response to Cardinal Ratzinger and a Warning to the Whole Church*. Minneapolis: Winston Press, 1985.

Sobrino, Jon. *Archbishop Romero: Memories and Reflections*. Maryknoll, NY: Orbis Books, 1990.

———. "Awakening from the Sleep of Inhumanity." *The Principle of Mercy: Taking the Crucified People from the Cross*. Maryknoll, NY: Orbis Books, 1994.

———. "A Civilization to Humanize a Gravely Ill World." Graduation Speech, Jesuit School of Theology of Santa Clara, May 24, 2014. Transcript in personal files of Robert Lassalle-Klein. Edited version published as "On the Way to Healing: Humanizing a Gravely Ill World." *America: The Jesuit Review*. November 10, 2014.

———. "A Su Aire." In Gómez-Oliver, Valentí, and Benítez, Josep M.; eds., *31 jesuítas se confiesan*. Lassalle-Klein, Robert, trans. Barcelona: Ediciones Península, 2003, 483–500.

———. "Carta a Ellacuría, El 'siempre' del pueblo crucificado. 'Qué hacer con los Buenos.' Dean Brackley." ["Letter to Ellacuría: The 'Always' of the Crucified People. 'What to Do with the Good Ones.' Dean Brackley"] *Carta a las Iglesias*. Año XXX, No. 618, 1–30 de octubre de 2011: 25–27.

———. *Christ the Liberator: A View from the Victims*. Maryknoll, NY: Orbis Books, 2001. Burns, Paul, trans. *La fe en*

Jesucristo: Ensayo desde las víctimas. San Salvador: UCA, 1999.

———. "Companions of Jesus." In Sobrino, Jon, Ellacuría, Ignacio, et al., eds. *Companions of Jesus: the Jesuit Martyrs of El Salvador.* Maryknoll, NY: Orbis Books, 1990.

———. "The Crucified Peoples: Yahweh's Suffering Servant Today." *The Principle of Mercy: Taking the Crucified People from the Cross.* Maryknoll, NY: Orbis Books, 1994, 49–57.

———. "Foreword, with Gratitude and Hope." In Robert Lassalle-Klein. *Blood and Ink: Ignacio Ellacuría, Jon Sobrino, and the Jesuit Martyrs of the University of Central America.* Maryknoll, NY: Orbis, 2014, xiii–xiv.

———. "Hablando con Jon Sobrino, Hacer Creible la Fe." *Mision Abierta.* Junio, No. 6 (1993): 6–9.

———. "Ignacio Ellacuría, the Human Being and the Christian." In Burke, Kevin F., and Lassalle-Klein, Robert, eds. *Love That Produces Hope: The Thought of Ignacio Ellacuría.* Collegeville, MN: Liturgical Press, 2006, 1–67.

———. *Jesus in Latin America.* Maryknoll, NY: Orbis Books, 1978. *Jesús in América Latina. Su significado para la fe y la cristología.* San Salvador: UCA Editores, 1982.

———. "Jesus of Galilee from the Salvadoran Context: Compassion, Hope, and Following the Light of the Cross." Lassalle-Klein, Robert, ed. *The Galilean Jesus.* Special Issue of *Theological Studies* 70, no. 2 (2009): 437–60.

———. *Jesus the Liberator: A Historical-Theological View.* Maryknoll, NY: Orbis Books, 1993. Burns, Paul, and McDonagh, Francis, trans. *Jesucristo liberador. Lectura histórica de Jesús de Nazaret.* San Salvador: UCA Editores, 1991.

———. "Karl Rahner and Liberation Theology." *The Way* 43, no. 44 (2004): 53–66.

———. "Letter to Hartono Budi, S.J., June 30, 1999." Lassalle-Klein, Robert, trans. San Salvador-Berkeley, CA. 30 de junio 1999. Transcript in personal files of Robert Lassalle-Klein. The Spanish original is included as an appendix in

Budi, Hartono. "The Christology of Jon Sobrino and Contemporary Martyrdom." Th.D. Thesis. Graduate Theological
Union & Jesuit School of Theology at Berkeley, CA, 1999.

———. "Letter to Fr. Peter Hans Kolvenbach." Lassalle-Klein,
Robert, trans. "Jon Sobrino al P. Peter Hans Kolvenbach, 13
de diciembre del 2006." Jon Sobrino, personal correspondence with Robert Lassalle-Klein (August 18, 2015). Transcript in personal files of Robert Lassalle-Klein.

———. "Maura, Ita, Dorothy, and Jean." In *Witnesses to the
Kingdom: The Martyrs of El Salvador and the Crucified
Peoples.* Maryknoll, NY, Orbis Books, 2003, 54–56. First
published in *Estudios Centroamericanos* January–February
1981: 51– 53. First English translation. Jon Sobrino, *Spirituality of Liberation.* Maryknoll, NY: Orbis Books, 1988,
153–56.

———. "Meditación ante el pueblo crucificado." *Sal Terrae* 74
(1986): 93–104.

———. "El padre Ellacuría sobre Monseñor Romero, ayudas
para poner a producir en las iglesias la herencia de Jesús."
Revista Latinoamericana de Teología 65 (2005): 117–37.

———. *The Principle of Mercy: Taking the Crucified People
from the Cross.* Maryknoll, NY: Orbis Books, 1994.

———. "Some Personal Reflections." In *Archbishop Romero:
Memories and Reflections.* Barr, Robert R., trans. Maryknoll, NY: Orbis Books, 1990, 2016.

———. *Spirituality of Liberation: Toward Political Holiness.*
Barr, Robert, trans. Maryknoll, NY: Orbis Books, 1988.

———. "Teología en un mundo sufriente: La teología de la liberación como 'intellectus amoris.'" *Revista Latinoamericana
de Teología* 15 (1988): 243–66.

———. *The True Church and the Poor.* Barr, Robert, trans.
Maryknoll, NY: Orbis Books, 1984.

Sobrino, Jon, Martín-Baró, I., and Cardenal, R. *La voz de los sin
voz: La palabra viva de Monseñor Oscar Arnulfo Romero.*
San Salvador: UCA Editores, 1980.

Sobrino, Jon, and Ellacuría, Ignacio. *Mysterium Liberationis: Fundamental Concepts of Liberation Theology.* Maryknoll, NY: Orbis Books, 1993.

Tracy, David. *Practical Theology: The Emerging Field in Theology, Church and World.* Browning, Don S., ed. New York: Harper and Row, 1983.

Trigo, Pedro. "Horizonte cristiano de la pastoral de la movilidad." *Revista Latinoamericana de Teología* 91 (2014): 3–39.

United Nations. "Press Conference by United Nations Special Rapporteur on Right to Food." October 26, 2007. https://www.un.org/press/en/2007/071026_Ziegler.doc.htm.

United States Jesuit Conference. *Documents of the 31st and 32nd General Congregations of the Society of Jesus.* St. Louis, MO: Institute of Jesuit Sources, 1977.

Zubiri, Xavier. *El hombre y Dios.* Madrid: Alianza Editorial, 1984.

MODERN SPIRITUAL MASTERS
Robert Ellsberg, Series Editor

This series introduces the essential writing and vision of some of the great spiritual teachers of our time. While many of these figures are rooted in long-established traditions of spirituality, others have charted new, untested paths. In each case, however, they have engaged in a spiritual journey shaped by the challenges and concerns of our age. Together with the saints and witnesses of previous centuries, these modern spiritual masters may serve as guides and companions to a new generation of seekers.

Already published:
Modern Spiritual Masters (edited by Robert Ellsberg)
Swami Abhishiktananda (edited by Shirley du Boulay)
Metropolitan Anthony of Sourozh (edited by Gillian Crow)
Eberhard Arnold (edited by Johann Christoph Arnold)
Pedro Arrupe (edited by Kevin F. Burke, S.J.)
Daniel Berrigan (edited by John Dear)
Thomas Berry (edited by Mary EvelynTucker and John Grim)
Dietrich Bonhoeffer (edited by Robert Coles)
Robert McAfee Brown (edited by Paul Crowley)
Dom Helder Camara (edited by Francis McDonagh)
Carlo Carretto (edited by Robert Ellsberg)
G. K. Chesterton (edited by William Griffin)
Joan Chittister (edited by Mary Lou Kownacki and Mary Hembrow Snyder)
Yves Congar (edited by Paul Lakeland)
The Dalai Lama (edited by Thomas A. Forsthoefel)
Alfred Delp, S.J. (introduction by Thomas Merton)
Catherine de Hueck Dogerty (edited by David Meconi, S.J.)
Virgilio Elizondo (edited by Timothy Matovina)
Jacques Ellul (edited by Jacob E. Van Vleet)
Ralph Waldo Emerson (edited by Jon M. Sweeney)
Charles de Foucauld (edited by Robert Ellsberg)
Mohandas Gandhi (edited by John Dear)
Bede Griffiths (edited by Thomas Matus)
Romano Guardini (edited by Robert A. Krieg)
Gustavo Gutiérrez (edited by Daniel G. Groody)
Thich Nhat Hanh (edited by Robert Ellsberg)
Abraham Joshua Heschel (edited by Susannah Heschel)

Etty Hillesum (edited by Annemarie S. Kidder)
Caryll Houselander (edited by Wendy M. Wright)
Pope John XXIII (edited by Jean Maalouf)
Rufus Jones (edited by Kerry Walters)
Clarence Jordan (edited by Joyce Hollyday)
Walter Kasper (edited by Patricia C. Bellm and Robert A. Krieg)
John Main (edited by Laurence Freeman)
James Martin (edited by James T. Keane)
Anthony de Mello (edited by William Dych, S.J.)
Thomas Merton (edited by Christine M. Bochen)
John Muir (edited by Tim Flinders)
John Henry Newman (edited by John T. Ford, C.S.C.)
Henri Nouwen (edited by Robert A. Jonas)
Flannery O'Connor (edited by Robert Ellsberg)
Karl Rahner (edited by Philip Endean)
Brother Roger of Taizé (edited by Marcello Fidanzio)
Richard Rohr (edited by Joelle Chase and Judy Traeger)
Oscar Romero (by Marie Dennis, Rennie Golden, and Scott Wright)
Joyce Rupp (edited by Michael Leach)
Albert Schweitzer (edited by James Brabazon)
Frank Sheed and Maisie Ward (edited by David Meconi)
Sadhu Sundar Singh (edited by Charles E. Moore)
Mother Maria Skobtsova (introduction by Jim Forest)
Jon Sobrino (edited by Robert Lassalle-Klein)
Dorothee Soelle (edited by Dianne L. Oliver)
Edith Stein (edited by John Sullivan, O.C.D.)
David Steindl-Rast (edited by Clare Hallward)
William Stringfellow (edited by Bill Wylie-Kellerman)
Pierre Teilhard de Chardin (edited by Ursula King)
Mother Teresa (edited by Jean Maalouf)
St. Thérèse of Lisieux (edited by Mary Frohlich)
Phyllis Tickle (edited by Jon M. Sweeney)
Henry David Thoreau (edited by Tim Flinders)
Howard Thurman (edited by Mary Krohlich)
Leo Tolstoy (edited by Charles E. Moore)
Evelyn Underhill (edited by Emilie Griffin)
Vincent Van Gogh (by Carol Berry)
Jean Vanier (edited by Carolyn Whitney-Brown)
Swami Vivekananda (edited by Victor M. Parachin)
Simone Weil (edited by Eric O. Springsted)
John Howard Yoder (edited by Paul Martens and Jenny Howells)